Be a Contender,
Not Just a Contestant!

To Ms. Eunice Harris; Brother
Parkman's best friend in
Augusta!

God bless you and cause
your way to be prosperous!
Keep the Faith and never
give up on God!
"Fight to Win!"

Kenneth D.

Be a Contender, Not Just a Contestant!

A Winning Strategy
For Achieving Spiritual Fitness and
Reaching Spiritual Maturity in Jesus Christ

Foreword by Chaplain Lonnie P. Williams Jr.
Introduction by Bishop F. D. Lawson Jr.

Reverend Kenneth L. Gainous

American Literary Press, Inc.
Five Star Special Edition
Baltimore, Maryland

Be a Contender, Not Just a Contestant!

Library of Congress
Cataloging in Publication Data
ISBN 1-56167-765-5

Library of Congress Card Catalog Number:
2002092942

Unless otherwise identified, Scripture quotations are from the King James version
of the Bible. Scripture quotations marked (NIV) and (NKJ) are from the *New
International Version* and the *New King James* versions of the Bible respectively.
Emphasis within Scripture quotes and underlined words are the author's own.

Published by

American Literary Press, Inc.
Five Star Special Edition
8019 Belair Road, Suite 10
Baltimore, Maryland 21236

Manufactured in the United States of America

Dedication

This glorious work is dedicated to my loving wife, Sharlotte, - our wonderful daughter, Ebony Nicole - my loving parents, Dr. Elizabeth C. Gainous and SGM (Ret.) Willie Gainous, Jr. - my big brother and hero, Willie Gainous, III - my wonderful in-laws, SFC (Ret.) Roy T. Davison (now resting in the Lord) and Ms. Bonnie M. Davison - my special cousin, Ms. Carolyn Curry-Bowen; my beloved relatives, dear friends and our precious church family at the Christian City of Praise (CCP)!

"To God Be the Glory for the things He has done!"

Acknowledgements

This work has benefited from review by a number of people, who gave generously of their time and spiritual knowledge to ensure that God's Glory and the integrity of scripture are revealed throughout this book. I would like to thank the following persons who reviewed part or all of the manuscript for publication: Reverend Mohandas M. Martin, Associate Minister, Christian City of Praise (CCP), Augusta, GA; Deacon James D. Scott, Jr., Deacon Ministry, First Baptist Church, Augusta, GA; Ms. Sandra K. Richardson, Tulsa, OK; and Mrs. Carol V. Hriczov, Suwanee, GA.

I am especially grateful for the following persons who contributed to this work by providing spiritual insights, endorsements, financial support, production support and written words of confirmation that have enhanced the message the Lord has given for me to share with the world. Thanks and special acknowledgements are rendered to Dr. Frank M. Reid, III, Senior Pastor, Bethel A.M.E. Church, Baltimore, MD; Mrs. Olivia Gavin, Assistant Youth Director, CCP, Augusta, GA; Mr. Robert Boone, Sr.; Minister of Music, CCP, Augusta, GA; Mr. Alan Mills (my cousin), Tampa, FL; Mr. and Mrs. Edward Hriczov, Suwanee, GA; Reverend Michael Turner and Sister Gale Turner, Associate Ministry team, ST Elmo Missionary Baptist Church, Lawton, OK; Chaplain Lonnie P. Williams, Jr., U.S. Army Chaplain Corps, Fort Lewis, WA; and Bishop F.D. Lawson, Jr., (my pastor, mentor and spiritual father in the ministry) Oklahoma City, OK.

I would also like to thank Ms. Donna Wessel and the professional staff at *American Literary Press, Inc.* for their exceptional work in producing this finished book for me. My selecting you to do this work has proven to be *a wise choice!* God bless you.

Contents

Foreword

God could not have given me a more beloved friend and "Brother in Christ" than Pastor Kenneth L. Gainous. I remember that day in Stillwater, Oklahoma, when we realized there was a life-long spiritual connection between us. We were part of a Student Christian Fellowship called ICF (Interdenominational Christian Fellowship). Often, the brothers of the fellowship would meet for prayer, bible study or simply to fellowship. On this particular evening, we were going into the apartment complex where we would meet. On the way, the group encountered a young man (student) who was intoxicated. Of course, our fellowship relished in the opportunity to witness for Christ. This would be the opportunity of a lifetime! Like a pack of wolves, we surrounded the student going for the spiritual kill. Well, to make a long story short, this encounter with the drunken student was hilarious! There we were, about 6-8 Christian brothers, surrounding and arguing with a drunken man about the existence of God. In the midst of this melee, Kenny and my eyes connected and seemed to say, "This is ridiculous – something's very wrong here!" Subsequently, we quieted the crowd, prayed for the young student and went on our way. This was the beginning of a relationship spanning some 20+ years. I've seen him in every aspect of which *"Be A Contender, Not Just A Contestant!"* speaks. Believe me, no one is more qualified to give the Body of Christ a new fresh perspective on the Christian life than he is.

Being challenged and battling against the enemy of our soul is the great constant for the people of God. It will continue as the Church moves in this new millennium attempting to be a beacon of light in a world increasingly overwhelmed by the opponents of darkness. We are facing an entirely different world than many of us, in the household of faith, could have ever imagined. This is why God's people must move with a sense of urgency and purpose. We must be aware of the battleground where the competitive war of light verses darkness; life verses death and hope verses despair is waged. Furthermore, in order to compete effectively in the kingdom of God, God's people must embrace the level of commitment and dedication needed to win for God the souls of humanity. That is the principal purpose of *"Be A Contender, Not Just A Contestant!"* In this regard, Pastor Gainous offers a wide range of spiritual insight, information and experience needed by the people of God at every level (Newborn Babes to Aged Saints) to raise their personal level of commitment.

This book does not consist of frivolous doctrinal ideas or archaic theological constructs. It's relevant and speaks to common experiences we all have. Pastor Gainous, with the precision of a battlefield commander (spiritual), interweaves his diverse history of athlete, soldier and pastor into a work easy to identify with. Powerful, grappling and enticing is Pastor Gainous' own story. It adds personal touches that allow readers to see themselves and realize his story is also theirs. These historical aspects, of his life, give him a unique perspective into the treasures of God's word. Every athlete, soldier, former athlete and yes, even spiritual couch potatoes will find his symbolism, analogies and illustrations simple but explosive! Every serious competitor understands what it takes to win. Every competitor understands what it takes to get there! Furthermore – in today's sports consumed culture, fans understand this as well! Fans appreciate the hard work and rejoice in the victory of the true competitor. Pastor Gainous, throughout this book, challenges us with this idea – "Why should the athlete of God be any different?" They should not is his word to the people of God! This is the simple but prolific message given the body of Christ: *"Be A Contender, Not Just A Contestant!"*

Finally – you must know, pastor Gainous is my brother and friend! However, what I appreciate most about him and what motivated me to do this foreword is the simple truth that for all the years we have known each other – he has lived the words of his book. He is *A Contender in the Body of Christ – Not Just A Contestant!* My hope for each of you is after reading this inspired word, you will raise your level of commitment for God and ***"Be A Contender, Not Just A Contestant!"***

Chaplain Lonnie P. Williams, Jr.
United States Army Chaplain

Introduction

Are you a contender or a contestant? This thought came to mind as I pondered a passage of scripture the Apostle Paul wrote in II Thessalonians 2:3, *"except there come a falling away..."* Paul accurately predicted and proclaimed that the last days would be marked, identified with and distinguished by a great *"falling away."* This prophetic word has become a reality. I'm thinking, how can there be such a falling away? The Lord spoke to me and reminded me of His words that are written in the Gospel of ST Mark, *"And you will be hated by all men for My name's sake. But he who endures to the end shall be saved."* (Mark 13:13) It is often said that the race is not given to the swift nor to the strong, but to the one who endures to the end. *Endurance* is a fundamental requirement in Christian doctrine and discipleship. Endure means to continue in the same state, to remain firm under suffering or misfortune *without yielding.* You endure when you holdout against the odds and continue maintaining your composure without giving in or up. The Apostle Paul said in II Timothy 4:3, *"the time will come when they will not endure sound doctrine..."* (NKJ) Christians must resolve in their heart to remain steadfast, unmovable and immutable in their faith and commitment to God, to the very end.

The Saints of God are like athletes competing in a grueling track race! Every believer must realize that the race of life is not a sprint race; *it's a marathon!* By definition, a marathon is a long-distance race, or a footrace that is run on open courses whose distance spans more than 26 miles. *A marathon is simply a contest of endurance!* It is an event or activity that requires prolonged and concentrated effort. The marathon participant who desires to win must commit to executing an intensive training program to prepare him or her for the race.

The Holy Bible instructs us to *"contend earnestly for the faith which was once for all delivered to the saints."* (Jude 1:3 NKJ) This book focuses on identifying the distinction between a *contender* and a *contestant.* A contender differs from a contestant in two major areas: *preparation and dedication.* Preparation, self-denial and commitment are the most differentiating characteristics between winners and losers.

In my conclusion, I encourage each of you to *"Be A Contender, Not Just A Contestant!"* Finish your course. Don't be a drop out. *A quitter never wins and a winner never quits!* Galatians 5:7 states *"You ran well. Who hindered you from obeying the truth?"* (NKJ) Meet every challenge with utmost confidence. Go forward with a positive attitude and always remember the encouraging words of the Apostle Paul, *"I can do all things through Christ who strengthens me."* (Ph. 4.13 NKJ)

It is with joy and it gives me great pleasure to speak a word on behalf of the author of this book. My acquaintance came while Pastor Gainous matriculated at Oklahoma State University, pursuing his goal of becoming a professional engineer. Having worshipped with us at Lawson's Temple Church Of God In Christ, *"The Little Friendly Church with the Family Atmosphere,"* I found him to be a devout Christian. His commitment to God was not secondary. He very studiously applied himself in maintaining a proper relationship with God while maintaining a high level of excellence as a student and soldier in the armed services. His background makes this text most interesting. I highly recommend this book to all progressive minded persons.

Bishop F. D. Lawson, Jr.
Oklahoma City, Oklahoma

Chapter I

WHO ARE YOU: A CONTENDER OR A CONTESTANT?

"Know ye not that they which run in a race run all, but one receiveth the prize? So run, that ye may obtain. And every man that striveth for the mastery is temperate in all things. Now they do it to obtain a corruptible crown; but we an incorruptible. I therefore so run, not as uncertainly; so fight I, not as one that beateth the air: But I keep under my body, and bring it into subjection: lest that by any means, when I have preached to others, I myself should be a castaway." **(1 Cor 9:24-27)**

We are living in a world that is filled with ordinary people like you and me who are struggling to make it and make ends meet on a daily basis. People, who are striving to overcome and endure all of the surprises and obstacles that seem to crop up at the most inopportune times in our lives. We constantly face problems and issues that demand our attention and resources right now, regardless of whether or not we are already totally engaged in other battles in our lives, or have the means available to satisfy them. The normal affairs of life are pressing enough without the added burdens or unforeseen contingencies that abruptly appear in the arena of our lives that present great challenges to our faith and peace with God. I often share with our congregation at the Christian City of Praise (CCP) that life is a giant roller coaster that is full of ups and downs, big loop-to-loops and tremendous turns. *Life is one big fight!* Yes, life is tough at times and has caused many people, *even believers in Jesus Christ,* to give up and surrender in the face of extreme adversity. However, today, the

1

Lord has instructed me to challenge you to "Be a contender, not just a contestant!"

The Lord has embedded this thought into my heart and spirit through the many obstacles and challenges that my family and I have overcome and conquered during the past twenty years that we have been serving God in ministry. We are products of unyielding faith and confidence in God! We have lived with a resolve to reveal the reality of God in this present world so that people everywhere can see and know that we serve the God of yesterday, today! *God wants you to know that you are a winner!* Never mind the battle scars that you are wearing because of the intensive warfare that you have been waging with Satan! *Wear your scars with dignity!* Never mind the fact that many times it seems that you are losing ground and falling behind the desired pace! *Just keep in step with God!* Don't listen to the voices of the countless many that will tell you to give up and concede defeat in cherished areas that you are pressing to win in your life! *Never give up on God!* The Lord told me to tell you that the only person that can make you a loser is you, because the Bible says, *"Ye are of God, little children, and have overcome them: because greater is he that is in you, than he that is in the world!"* (I Jn 4:4) Faithless people give faithless advice! Listen to and follow the Spirit of God, stand on the Word of God, trust in the Mercy of God, expect to receive the Grace of God and you will always finish a winner and not just a contestant! *Hallelujah! Praise the Lord!*

God wants all of us to be contenders, not just a contestant! *Contestants* are a dime a dozen. The *contenders* represent a very small population of the total number of participants. Webster's Dictionary defines a contestant as being "a person who takes part in a contest." By this definition, a *contestant* is no more than a competitor or participant in a race, an event or an affair. It doesn't take much to be a contestant. Often times you don't have to have any special gift or talent. Sometimes all you have to do is simply show up, sign your name, pay an entry fee and you will qualify as a contestant. A *contender* is a person who is not only in the race or

2

competition, but is considered to have a legitimate chance and opportunity to win the race! A contender possesses the ability and potential to win and conquer his or her opponent.

The old saints of God used the saying, *"every now and then, a traveler,"* to describe the infrequency of journeymen that actually travel on the contender's highway. In the seventh chapter of ST. Matthew, Jesus used the illustration of the broad way and the narrow way to communicate a message to his disciples and inform them of the distinguishing differences between the contestant's road and the contender's road. Jesus encouraged his disciples and challenged them when he said, *"Enter through the narrow gate. For wide is the gate and broad is the road that leads to destruction, and many enter through it. But small is the gate and narrow the road that leads to life, and only a few find it."* (Matt 7:13-14 NIV) Now observe, both roads are legitimate and have travelers on them. However, the roads are distinguished from the other by their entry point, physical size, population, and ultimate destination. This in essence is the heart of the message. God's way is the way of the abundant life and *few believers* will ever enjoy it. The contestant's way is filled with a consortium of people who represent a carnal culture that feeds into the mainstream of satisfying the cravings of our sinful flesh. The Apostle John warned the believers concerning seeking fulfillment from the things of the world and said, *"Do not love the world or anything in the world. If anyone loves the world, the love of the Father is not in him. For everything in the world-- the cravings of sinful man, the lust of his eyes and the boasting of what he has and does-- comes not from the Father but from the world. The world and its desires pass away, but the man who does the will of God lives forever."* (I Jn 2:15-17 NIV) However, even with this sound advice from the beloved apostle, we find that most believers are only contestants who are hopelessly locked in on worldly prizes and never live in the victory of Jesus Christ nor realize the true blessings of God's salvation.

Let us consider the Boston Marathon to establish the difference using a real world example. First of all, the Boston Marathon is one of the most prestigious distance-running events in the world. Representatives from across the continuum seek to participate in the race each year. Over 15,000 runners register annually as valid contestants or participants in the race, but only about 10 are considered to be legitimate contenders to win the race, *before the race is even run!* Sports casters interview the contenders prior to the race to gain insights concerning their strategies and tactics they will employ to win the race. Consequently, only the elite in the total number will be offered an interview before the race and even fewer actually get an interview after the race is finished. There may be many contestants, but there are normally only a few legitimate contenders! Who are you today? Are you a contender or a contestant? Let's bring the point home. *Above all things, who are you in the Lord and what are you doing to make the cause of Christ successful?* Are you simply a church member, or a living witness for Jesus Christ? Are you a Christian Contender, or a religious contestant? You make the call!

STOP! Before you make the call, I want to give you a brief contrast between a contender and a contestant. Maybe this will enlighten you and assist you in defining who you are spiritually. I will use a direct comparison between the two categories of people to make my point.

1. First of all, *a contender has a strong and impeccable work ethic.* He or she is totally committed to making personal sacrifices in order to keep the winning edge through tough training programs and killer-workouts. *A contestant is lazy and complacent in training,* and does not make the sacrifices that are needed to raise his or her competitive level. Jesus told his followers that in order to be his disciple, you must first *"deny yourself, take up your cross daily and follow me."* (Mt. 16.24) True discipleship is a life of personal denial and constant sacrifice. Few people are willing to live at that level on a continuous basis. However, if you are

willing, there is no limit to what God will do in you and through you to bless the people around you!

2. *A contender maintains his or her focus, has a good competitive strategy and plans to win.* A contender never enters any competitive event without first planning for the event and developing a good strategy to employ throughout the competition. *A contestant fails to plan and therefore plans to fail.* Contestants think-on-the-fly and plan-as-they-go! Every believer needs to know and understand that your plan is centered on the vision that God gives you, to keep you focused during the clouded moments of intensive spiritual warfare. Strategies differ from event to event but they all are designed to accomplish the same end, *WINNING!*

3. *A contender is committed to achieving Excellence in every event and competition.* A contender maximizes his or her potential to perform and compete at the highest level. He or she is driven by the desire to be the best in the bunch! *A contestant accepts Mediocrity and is satisfied with where he or she is, regardless if it is at the bottom.* Spiritual Excellence is the standard of God for all of His children. Paul challenged every believer to *"press towards the goal for the prize of the upward call of God in Christ Jesus."* (Phil. 3.14 NKJ) There is no room for mediocrity in the ministry of God! *Nothing about God is mediocre!* He is a great God and a great Savior and He demands a great commitment from all of His people to achieve *Excellence in Ministry!*

4. *A contender knows that he or she can win and is always prepared for their opponent.* The contenders have confidence because they have studied their opponent thoroughly, become very familiar with the opponent's strengths, weaknesses, capabilities and threats that they pose to the contender. Simply speaking, they have trained adequately to win the contest! *A contestant hopes to win and seldom meets the opponent's challenge.* It goes back to the very first point that we made concerning a contestant. *A contestant is lazy and complacent in training,* and does not make the sacrifices that are needed to raise his or her competitive level.

Therefore, a contestant does not have confidence in his or her ability to win against a legitimate foe. He or she does not study their opponent and usually fails to train to the appropriate level to win. Paul said in our key scripture, *"Do you not know that those who run in a race all run, but one receives the prize? Run in such a way that you may obtain it."* (1 Cor 9:24 NKJ) Every believer should enter each spiritual event or competition with the assurance that they will be victorious! The Saints of God must always remember that we war and compete with Divine assistance through the presence of God and the power of the Holy Ghost! Paul said, *"If God be for us, who can be against us?"* (Rom. 8.31 NKJ) *"I can do all things through Christ who strengthens me."* (Phil. 4.13 NKJ)

Let me close this portion of our discussion by sharing some personal observations concerning spiritual contestants and mediocre Christians in ministry. *Spiritual Contestants and Mediocre Christians* never volunteer for the tough jobs in ministry. They will not and cannot go out into the neighborhoods to witness one-on-one with unbelievers. They never can or will pray in a great company and always get nervous when there is a need for someone to fill in to teach a spiritual lesson. They are afraid to witness at work or in the presence of unbelievers and habitually join in the telling and sharing of questionable jokes. They always want to fit in with the crowd and never want to make any waves, even if it jeopardizes their witness for Jesus Christ. *Spiritual Contestants and Mediocre Christians* always have an excuse for why they did not show up for Bible Study, Sunday school, morning worship services, prayer meetings, women's fellowship and brotherhood meetings. The only time they receive from God is when they come to Sunday service. They never study the Word of God on their own and are ignorant of the most basic scriptures that all believers should know to overcome the attacks of the devil. In essence, *Spiritual Contestants and Mediocre Christians* live defeated lives, are never really satisfied in their personal lives and always depend on other *"strong believers"* to pull them through during spiritual crises. *Now, where do YOU stand?* Are you a *contender* or a *contestant?* <u>*YOU MAKE THE CALL!*</u>

I had to make the call in my personal life and acknowledge that I was a spiritual failure to God because I did nothing to promote or advance the Kingdom of God on this earth! I could not witness to anyone because I was ignorant of His word and knew nothing about the power of the Holy Spirit! I could not show people the way because my lifestyle was contrary to the way of God's holiness. *I made the call in my life* when I realized that my goodness was not good enough. Going to church and being a morally good person with manners was not enough for God. The unsaved people in the world can accomplish that! The devil is telling every believer to be religious and moral because he knows that religion and morals will not save anyone! Religion is killing people in the church today and stopping the free movement of the Spirit of God in our worship services. Religion is nothing more than *legalism* in the church, and legalism is the obstacle that prevents us from enjoying liberty and freedom in the Lord! *Righteousness* is what God is seeking to produce through the lives of His children! Proverbs 14:34 says that *"Righteousness exalteth a nation: but sin is a reproach to any people."* God is demanding a *total surrender* to His way and ideas concerning life. God does not want us to be natural *He wants us to be supernatural!* Jesus said in Luke 10:19, *"Behold, I give unto you power to tread on serpents and scorpions, and over all the power of the enemy: and nothing shall by any means hurt you."* The Word of God says *"We are more than conquerors through him that loved us."* (Rom 8:37) *Praise the name of the Lord!* God wants us to be Christian contenders for Him in the world! *We are winners to the Glory of God!* *YOU ARE A WINNER!* *You are not average!* *You are exceptional!* *HALLELUJAH!*

Bishop F.D. Lawson, Jr. inspired me to write this book. He planted this seed of faith in me over twenty years ago when I was a young college student at Oklahoma State University in Stillwater, OK. He used this same subject, *"Be a Contender, Not Just a*

7

Contestant," to communicate a message to me that has changed my life and my entire approach to worshipping and serving the Lord. That seed that he planted in me years ago has been watered by faith and has grown through my experiences and walk with the Lord of Glory. That same seed of the Word of God has been developed in me and has made me a determined warrior for Jesus Christ. Bishop Lawson's message impacted me in an eternal manner and has motivated me to be an ambassador and witness for my Savior everywhere I go.

It is amazing what the *truth* will do for you, if you will receive it. Jesus said, *"If ye continue in my word, then are ye my disciples indeed; And ye shall know the truth, and the truth shall make you free."* (John 8:31-32) We must be lovers of the truth and be able to come to the knowledge of the truth if we are going to be used by God. The truth of God's word will liberate us from the bondage and guilt of sin. My brothers and sisters, the devil puts us in bondage when he convinces us that we have nothing to offer God but our Sunday service. The devil puts us in bondage when he convinces us that we have nothing to give in the Lord's service but our money. The devil puts us in bondage when he convinces us that we are too tired to make it out to Bible Study, Sunday school, or even *too tired at night* and *running too late in the morning* to spend personal time with the Lord in a devotional period. It is the truth that makes us free! The truth of God makes us powerful! Jesus prayed to the Father for Him to *"Sanctify them through thy truth: thy word is truth."* (John 17:17) Jesus said in John 15:3, *"Now ye are clean through the word which I have spoken unto you."* This lets me know that the only way that we will ever be clean is through the Word of God and truly acknowledging where we are in Him. The Lord is encouraging us to *come clean, take off the show-face and see who we really are in the mirror of His Word. Are you a contender, or a contestant?*

If you are not actively involved in your church ministry and efforts to evangelize the unsaved people in your local community, you are living at the level of mediocrity and are no more than a contestant in the body of Christ. I am pleading with you, *YES YOU,* to rise up and be who Christ has called you to be! The Bible says of the saints of God, *"ye are a chosen generation, a royal priesthood, an holy nation, a peculiar people; that YE SHOULD shew forth the praises of him who hath called you out of darkness into his marvellous light:"* (1 Pet 2:9) Jesus said, *"Ye are the light of the world. A city that is set on an hill cannot be hid. Neither do men light a candle, and put it under a bushel, but on a candlestick; and it giveth light unto all that are in the house. Let your light so shine before men, that they may see your good works, and glorify your Father which is in heaven."* (Matt 5:14-16) The life of the Christian contender is a life that is spent living to glorify God. Peter reminded the Saints of God that we all have an important part to play in the evangelistic movement of God in the world. In 1 Pet 4:10-11 he stated, *"As every man hath received the gift, even so minister the same one to another, as good stewards of the manifold grace of God. If any man speak, let him speak as the oracles of God; if any man minister, let him do it as of the ability which God giveth: THAT GOD IN ALL THINGS MAY BE GLORIFIED THROUGH JESUS CHRIST, to whom be praise and dominion for ever and ever. Amen."* What are you doing for Jesus? Are you a *contender* or a *contestant?* <u>*YOU MAKE THE CALL!*</u>

Jesus is calling all of us to fulfill the great commission! Nobody is exempt from this command that He gave to His followers in Matthew 28:19-20, *"Go ye therefore, and teach all nations, baptizing them in the name of the Father, and of the Son, and of the Holy Ghost: Teaching them to observe all things whatsoever I have commanded you: and, lo, I am with you alway, even unto the end of the world. Amen."* We can make it and we can do it because He has promised to be with us! ***"Be a Contender, Not Just a Contestant!"***

Chapter II

HOW CAN I BECOME A CHRISTIAN CONTENDER?

Now that you have made the call in your personal life and have determined that you are a contestant and desire to become a contender for the Lord, let me share some thoughts concerning the way to accomplish your goal! I know that my way is effective because it has worked for a number of friends that I have shared this strategy with over the past several years. *It also works for me!* In fact, I received it from the Lord at a time when He enlightened me concerning the serious spiritual problems we were facing in our local church fellowship with carnality and sin growing within the body of Christ. These tips are designed to give you a leverage that will enable you to pull yourself up from the mundane lifestyle that the devil has subtly convinced you to live and empower you to rise above the level of mediocrity to achieve Christian maturity in the Lord.

Many times people identify deficiencies in our personal lives and reveal shortcomings that they feel hinder us from experiencing the power and the movement of God. I think one of the worst things anyone can do to me is identify flaws in my life without giving me a recommended solution to resolve them, or encouragement to overcome them. I never will forget my military days in the Army and the down-to-earth lessons I learned as a young commissioned officer from seasoned non-commissioned officers (NCOs) and veterans whom I have served with. I remember my First Sergeant (1SG Edmond L. Pankey) telling me one day, "LT (short for lieutenant) never criticize the performance or efforts of anyone unless it is constructive criticism. The only way any criticism can be constructive is if you share it with the right attitude and provide a recommended solution. DO NOT

11

FORGET THAT! You will make it if you remember that." In other words, you must be mindful of what you say, and more importantly, the way you say it. The Bible teaches us to be wise in our sharing with others, especially when it involves a negative point. Proverbs 11:30 says, *"The fruit of the righteous is a tree of life; and he that winneth souls is wise."* The Apostle Paul said in Galatians 6:1, *"Brethren, if a man be overtaken in a fault, ye which are spiritual, restore such an one in the spirit of meekness; considering thyself, lest thou also be tempted."* In the same spirit of that wise counsel, the Lord has given me some spiritual nuggets to share with you to help you on your road to becoming a contender for Jesus Christ.

1. YOU MUST FIRST BE SAVED and HUNGRY!

The first and most important step to becoming a Christian contender is experiencing God's great salvation. *You must be born again!* (JN. 3.3-6) Now you may think this is a given, and it should be. However, you would be surprised at the number of church people who hold positions of authority within our fellowships who are not saved. They have been permitted to serve in the church because of their secular clout or worldly status. Unsaved people cannot propel the church into the next level through natural means. It takes the Spirit of God to move the church forward and upward in the Lord! Jesus said, *"It is the spirit that quickeneth; the flesh profiteth nothing: the words that I speak unto you, they are spirit, and they are life."* (John 6:63) The Holy Spirit must be resident in you to enable you to accomplish the will of God, which is spiritual excellence!

Secondly, you must have a spiritual appetite! YOU MUST BE HUNGRY! Jesus said, *"Blessed are they which do hunger and thirst after righteousness: for they shall be filled."* (MT. 5.6) Hunger is desire and you must have a strong desire to please God in order to become a Christian contender. You must have a burning desire to be strong in the Lord! It doesn't just happen; *it*

12

must be in you to make it happen! I shared with my church family in a sermon that I preached a few months ago that you must at times develop an appetite for certain foods that will benefit your body and enable you to grow and maintain good health. Several years ago, I was diagnosed with hypertension, high blood pressure, at the young age of thirty. I found out that it is hereditary and it runs in my family on my mother's side. I did not have any visible symptoms or signs of the condition, nor did I feel bad or faint. I have always been very athletic from my youth and was a three-year high school All-State athlete in track and field, in the state of Oklahoma. I played football and basketball too and maintained a very high level of physical fitness throughout my high school and college years. However, when I joined the Army and stopped my intensive physical training, I began losing my high level of conditioning and sure enough the high blood pressure surfaced and became more evident as I grew older. When that happened, the doctor put me on medication and informed me that I would need to change my diet, stop eating all of those juicy cheese burgers, hot dogs, fried chicken dinners, red velvet cakes and all of the delicious foods that I love to eat! I also had to give up my chocolate milk shakes and Braums ice cream desserts. He then told me that I needed to cut the salt and begin eating more healthy foods like fruits and garden salads, baked chicken, grilled fish, steamed vegetables and every other tasteless food that I deemed horrible to consume. What is my point? The point is this: I had to acquire a taste and an appetite for the healthy foods, over a period of time. It was not easy, but I succeeded in doing so because I knew that it would benefit me and reduce my chances of developing heart disease or suffer a stroke down the road. Whereas I used to go to Burger King and order a Whopper with cheese value meal with French fries and a chocolate shake; I now order a side salad and a chocolate pie! I know that the pie is not healthy, but it really does a good job of killing the rest of my appetite and appeasing my sweet tooth! Nevertheless, I have acquired the taste for salads and fruit and the other healthy foods.

13

Whereas I used to eat fat filled foods for breakfast like doughnuts, pancakes and waffles, bacon, sausage and eggs and whole milk; now I enjoy Frosted Mini-Wheats, bananas, fruit bars and I use non-fat milk. Why? Because I have acquired a taste for them and they are healthy for me!

Well, praise the Lord! Today, the Saints of God must *acquire a spiritual appetite for the Word of God* in order for them to grow spiritually and increase their Faith and output for the Lord! You must have *a craving appetite for the Word of God* in order to experience and achieve spiritual maturity in the Lord! There is no such thing as a healthy baby, child or adult that will not eat! When our infants fail to eat and begin losing weight, we immediately take them to the doctor because we know that it is not normal for any growing child to lose their appetite. The only people who do not have an appetite are the ones who are stuffed to the brim because they just finished a good meal, those who are sick and need medical attention, and dead folks. *Do you have a healthy appetite for God's Holy Word?* If not, you probably are not a contender, you are most likely a contestant!

Let me make another observation or share some thoughts concerning this issue of spiritual maturity among the believers. The church is facing a crisis in the sense that there are so many spiritually weak and dysfunctional Christians within the body of Christ that a significant amount of our effort and energy is being expended trying to keep them alive and well! Carnal Christians who do not have a true desire to mature in the Lord literally fill our fellowships and hinder the progress of reaching the lost for Jesus! In many instances, these weak Christians become liabilities rather than spiritual assets. The Apostle Peter said, *"As newborn babes, desire the sincere milk of the word, that ye may grow thereby."* (I Pet. 2.2) *YOU CANNOT GROW WITHOUT THE WORD!* Many church fellowships today are no more than spiritual nurseries! Do not get me wrong. We need spiritual babies to be born every day in order to increase the body of Christ and continue the Godly heritage in the world! Moreover, they will be born if the Saints of

14

God will remain committed to fulfilling the Great Commission of Jesus Christ that He revealed in Matthew 28 verses 18-20! However, we need the babies to grow up and out of the spiritual nursery so that other babies can be born again! Think about it. Especially today, many of our community hospital facilities and medical centers' prenatal wards are overwhelmed and have demands that exceed their capacity to deliver all of the expectant mothers. Some expectant mothers have to be transferred from their normal medical facility to other hospitals to insure a safe and healthy delivery! New mothers are literally pulled up and pushed out of their rooms within two days of delivery and are sent home to recover and care for their newborn infants, *to make room for others!* There is not enough space to permit them to experience or enjoy the traditional three to five day delivery timeline that was the standard during earlier years. New babies are being born everyday and need room for delivery! Likewise, *hallelujah,* there is a harvest of ripe souls in the world that are waiting to be delivered to the Glory of God and we need to make room for them in our spiritual delivery area! The nursery is designed to be a transitional area, not a place to drop an anchor! We must ensure that everyone that is born into the Kingdom of God is nurtured in the Word and fed the spiritual bread from heaven that will promote and spur spiritual growth.

Also, think of the importance of a good meal. A healthy meal provides all of the nutrients and vitamins that our bodies need to grow and function properly. Likewise, the Holy Scriptures provide the spiritual nutrients and substance that are needed to facilitate healthy growth in the individual members and the collective body of Jesus Christ. That is why the Master asked Peter the questions concerning his love for Him in John 21 verses 15-17 and commanded him to prove his love when he said, *"Simon, son of Jonas, do you love me more than these?'* If you do, then '*Feed my lambs and feed my sheep."* Feeding and consuming wholesome meals are essential to promote healthy growth, both physically and spiritually.

15

Let me close this portion of our prescription for becoming a Christian contender by reminding you that Jesus said, *"It is written, Man shall not live by bread alone, but by every word that proceedeth out of the mouth of God."* (MT. 4.4) Therefore, we cannot live or experience the abundant life of God outside of the Word of God! Peter made a defining statement concerning our spiritual maturity when he encouraged the Saints of God to *"grow in grace, and in the knowledge of our Lord and Savior Jesus Christ...."* (2 PET. 3.18) When I grew up as a member of the youth department in my former church, our youth motto was *"let us grow, go and glow for Jesus Christ!"* That is the true challenge for every believer: to *grow, go and glow for Jesus Christ!* Job said, *"My foot hath held His steps, His way have I kept, and not declined. Neither have I gone back from the commandment of His lips; I have esteemed the words of His mouth more than my necessary food."* (Job 23. 11-12) If you are going to position yourself to answer the call to become a Christian contender for Jesus Christ, *YOU MUST FIRST BE SAVED and HUNGRY!* These are the most critical ingredients that are needed to reach the status of being a contender for Jesus Christ. Therefore, I have spent a lot of time with this section. If you cannot qualify at this entry point, you will not do the remaining requirements. They all are built upon the foundation of salvation and hunger for the Word. If you are willing to pass this first requirement, then *lets go on to the next one!*

2. TRAIN HARD!

Training is the key to winning in any great competition. I have served in the military, the active Army and United States Army Reserves for over twenty years and I have undergone extensive training to prepare me to perform my duties as a battalion commander. There is no substitute for training when it comes to preparing your unit to fight and survive on the battlefield. I commanded a tactical Signal company in Ludwigsburg, West

16

Germany that deployed from Stuttgart, Germany with the VII Corps (US) to support Operations Desert Shield and Desert Storm during the Persian Gulf War. Before we deployed, we trained and trained and trained over and over again to ensure that we could successfully perform our Mission Essential Task List (METL), to the prescribed standard, which outlined our unit's wartime mission. We also conducted survivability training involving individual and collective tasks that would increase our probability of surviving in the austere desert environment that we would encounter in Saudi Arabia, Iraq and the surrounding areas. I had several soldiers that were afraid of the thought of going to war because of the news reports that were published on CNN that spoke of the minefields, razor concertina wire, firetraps, SCUD missile attacks, chemical agents and the other destructive measures the Iraqis employed to stop our forces. However, I praise God that I had been blessed to have already served in combat arms units that routinely trained year round to conquer and overcome the obstacles that the Iraqi army employed against our forces! My training experience with these great units, the 2-37th Armor Battalion (Vilseck, Germany) and the 3-18th Field Artillery Battalion (Fort Sill, OK), enabled me to dispel my soldiers' doubts and assure them that our forces would not have any problems overcoming the tactical obstacles the Iraqis would use against us.

Now you may be asking yourself this question, "how does this fit into the formula for transforming me into a Christian contender?" I am glad you asked! The answer is simple. If you do not train hard in the Lord's Army, you will become a casualty of spiritual warfare! Untrained Christians are unskilled and will not endure the heat of battle against Satan and his army. *You must be trained to win!* All good soldiers are trained to survive and endure the most challenging circumstances and conditions during conflict on the battlefield. They know the difference between a war zone and a safe area. Just in case you did not know, *we are living in a spiritual war zone,* not a playground! The Apostle Paul said in his letter to the Ephesians, *"Finally, my brethren, be strong in the Lord and in the power of His might. Put on the whole armor of God, that you may be able to stand against the wiles of the devil. For we do not wrestle against flesh and blood, but against principalities, against powers, against the rulers of the darkness of this age, against spiritual hosts of wickedness in the heavenly places. Therefore take up the whole armor of God, that you may be able to withstand in the evil day..."* (Eph. 6:10-13 NKJ) We, the children of the Living God, must be trained at a level that will enable us to endure the fiery trials and darts of the devil. Contestants do not survive on the spiritual battlefield! They give up and voluntarily become spiritual prisoners of war (S-POWs)! The Apostle Paul knew the importance of strengthening the Saints of God and exhorted Timothy to *"be strong in the grace that is in Christ Jesus'* and challenged him to *'endure hardness, as a good soldier of Jesus Christ."* (2 TIM. 2.1,3)

Please allow me to use another illustration to communicate my point on training. Great athletes train extremely hard for two primary reasons: 1) to increase their ability to perform in the competition; and 2) to maximize their potential to win the competition!   They frequent the local training facilities and gymnasiums on a regular basis to execute workouts and training strategies that are designed to make them winners!   Your performance in any competition is directly related to the quality of your workout and the commitment that you put forth in training. I have a cousin that played professional baseball for the Baltimore Orioles. His name is Alan Mills. Alan actually played in the major league for over ten years as a middle relief pitcher. That is one of the toughest jobs in baseball. He usually entered the game when it is all messed up (e.g. the bases are loaded; no outs; and the top of the opposing team's order is coming up). Any way, Alan has shed some spiritual light to me concerning the commitment that is needed in training at the professional level that I have learned to apply in my spiritual walk with the Lord. Although the baseball season usually ends in October and does not reconvene until February, Alan never stops training. When I asked him why

18

he could not take a few weeks off to just relax and visit me in Georgia, he simply told me that he couldn't afford to go any substantial period of time without training because it will degrade his conditioning. *Conditioning is the purpose and objective of all athletic training!* Conditioning determines your stamina, toughness and power during the competitive event. Your level of conditioning determines your ability to withstand the rigors of impact sports and minimizes your potential for sustaining injuries. A good workout promotes physical and mental conditioning!

Well, let me close this section with this thought. *THE CHURCH AND YOUR HOME ARE YOUR SPIRITUAL GYMNASIUMS!* We train and get our spiritual conditioning at the Church during our worship services, our Sunday school and Bible study sessions. Likewise, we receive spiritual conditioning at home during our personal Bible studies and our quiet time with the Lord! We all must implement a good spiritual workout that will enhance our spiritual conditioning! *"STUDY & PRAYER": that's the Christian workout!* Study the Word of God and Pray everyday! That is what the Apostle Paul told Timothy and the church in Thessalonica to do in II Timothy 2.15 and I Thessalonians 5.17. He commanded Timothy to *"Study to shew thyself approved unto God, a workman that needeth not to be ashamed, rightly dividing the word of truth."* He challenged the Thessalonians to *"Pray without ceasing."*

Finally, another key training strategy that is often used by the most successful athletes is RESISTANCE TRAINING! *RESISTANCE BUILDS STRENGTH AND TOUGHNESS!* We must be resilient and resistant to the attacks of the devil in order to win the spiritual war! James exhorted the church to practice resistance training when he encouraged them to *"Submit yourselves therefore to God. Resist the devil, and he will flee from you."* (Ja. 4.7) I encourage you to *TRAIN HARD* so that you will be competitive in the war against the devil! Do not accept nor execute light workouts that do challenge you to reach down and pull something from within to accomplish the training or reach your spiritual objectives. There are always indicators to let me know when I have completed a good workout. *I am usually tired and aching.* If your physical workout does not press you and leave you exhausted after you are finished, then you really have not done a beneficial one. Consequently, if your *spiritual workout* does not leave you challenged to do more for Jesus and give you the desire to become more like Him, then you have not done a beneficial one. *TRAIN HARD!*

3. MAINTAIN YOUR SPIRITUAL DISCIPLINE!

HOLINESS is the discipline of God for all of His children! I often share with my congregation at CCP and the Saints of God everywhere that Holiness is not a jump or shout. It is not a plain face or certain physical look. *True Holiness* is the lifestyle of God flowing through the believer! Simply stated, Holiness is a disciplined life. Good discipline used to be the foundation upon which everything in our society was built. The discipline started in the home and permeated through our society. Children obeyed, honored and respected their parents and other adults. Discipline was the rule in our communities and it provided an environment that was free of most undesirable or criminal acts. Good discipline was instilled within the people in the community. This made the neighborhoods safe and dispelled fear of harm. Today, *discipline is a scarcity* in our homes and communities. Our society is failing at the foundation because discipline is a scarcity. Our children's schools are no longer safe from violence and criminal activity because of the increase in number of undisciplined children who attend them. The teachers have been stripped of the power and authority that is needed to maintain discipline in their classrooms. The only hope and refuge in the world today from the effects of sin is found in Jesus Christ and Holiness!

Spiritual discipline begins and has its root in obedience! In the Old Testament, Saul, the anointed king of Israel, faltered in discipline and it cost him his throne. God gave him explicit

20

instructions to *"go and smite Amalek, and utterly destroy all that they have, and spare them not; but slay both man and woman, infant and suckling, ox and sheep, camel and ass."* (I Sam. 15.3) Those were detailed instructions that could not be misconstrued or misunderstood. However, Saul lost his discipline, failed to carry out God's divine command and ruined his heritage as the king of Israel. Although he won the battle that day and conquered king Agag and the Amalekites, ultimately he lost the war and his relationship with God. The Prophet Samuel told Saul, *"Hath the Lord as great delight in burnt offerings and sacrifices, as in obeying the voice of the Lord? Behold, to obey is better than sacrifice, and to hearken than the fat of rams. For rebellion is as the sin of witchcraft, and stubbornness is as iniquity and idolatry. Because thou hast rejected the word of the Lord, he hath also rejected thee from being king."* (I Sam. 15. 22-23) What a price to pay for some personal glory! You will need to read the entire fifteenth chapter of I Samuel to get the full impact of this point. What do we learn from Saul's failure? Two things: 1) We must hear, receive and believe the instructions of the Lord and fulfill His commands in our lives at all times. 2) You must maintain your spiritual discipline above all other desires for personal gain and glory. These two principles will keep you in the way of God's blessing because the blessings of God are realized through obedience! The Lord told Isaiah to tell Israel, *"If you be willing and obedient, ye shall eat the good of the land:"* (Is. 1.19)

The contestant is not disciplined enough to comply with God's commands when they interfere with his or her personal agenda. Contestants do not possess the regimen that is needed to experience peace in chaotic and threatening circumstances. They do not have a heart to obey, or faith to follow when they do not understand or agree with the direction and command of God. Saints of God, you must be rooted and grounded in the Lord to display spiritual discipline when everything around you is falling apart and destruction is staring you in the face. Nothing can challenge the resolve of a disciplined soldier of Jesus Christ! The

21

Apostle Paul declared his willingness to lose all so that he would fulfill his purpose for Jesus Christ in the world. Paul said, *"And now, behold, I go bound in the spirit unto Jerusalem, not knowing the things that shall befall me there: Save the Holy Ghost witnesseth in every city, saying that bonds and afflictions abide me. But none of these things move me, neither count I my life dear unto myself, so that I might finish my course with joy, and the ministry, which I have received of the Lord Jesus, to testify the gospel of the grace of God."* (Acts 20.22-24) Paul was a disciplined soldier for Jesus Christ! What is your spiritual status in the Lord as it relates to discipline? Can you declare your willingness to lose all that Christ may win? If you can, you are a contender for Jesus Christ!

Paul said in I Corinthians 9 verse 24, *"Know ye not that they which run in a race run all, but one receiveth the prize? So run, that ye may obtain."* Paul uses illustrations from a Grecian contest to communicate a spiritual message to the church. Do not just be a participant in the event! Strive to be the champion! The word *"obtain"* literally means to seize, possess and apprehend. Winning is the goal of every true champion! The contender follows a strategy and training program that demands strict discipline in every facet to realize and *"obtain"* the victory. Paul went on to say in verse 25, *"And every man that striveth for the mastery is temperate in all things. Now they do it to obtain a corruptible crown; but we an incorruptible."* The key words in this 25th verse are *"striveth"* and *"temperate"*. To strive is to fight and to labor fervently! The Greek definition for *striveth* suggests a struggle to obtain or win a prize. In essence, the Christian's efforts in the competition cause him or her to contend with and to struggle against an adversary in order to accomplish a goal. Paul calls it *"the mastery"*. Paul also stated that *"temperance"* is required in the believer to be successful in obtaining the mastery. *Temperate* in this scripture means to be self-disciplined and to display self-control. Proverbs 25:28 says, *"He that hath no rule over his own spirit is like a city that is broken down, and without walls."* In other words, if you cannot control your temper and you always fly off the handle when things do not follow the logical order, you will be ruined and will ruin your witness for Jesus Christ in the world! Any Saint of God that has a bad temper is nothing more than a contestant because they are constantly open and unprotected against Satan's attacks: *"like a city that is broken down, and without walls."* *Temperance* is one of the nine fruit of the Spirit that are listed in Galatians 5. 22-23. Christian contenders maintain their composure, even in the heat of the battle because they possess the discipline that is required to *"wait on the Lord"* and they are *"filled with the Spirit of God!"* Spirit filled believers are spiritually mature Christians who hold onto the truth of God and maintain a disciplined spirit at all times, regardless of the events or circumstances that challenge their peace. If you are a Saint of God with a bad temper, you need to pray for deliverance today! Satan will set you up, place you in situations on your job, in the community, and even at your house that will set you off and cause you to blow up in front of the world. When this happens, it is hard to convince anyone that you are a child of the King. *Put that temper in check ASAP before it destroys you!*

The Word of God says, *"Be angry, and sin not: let not the sun go down upon your wrath: Neither give place to the devil."* (Eph. 4.26-27) The writer of Ecclesiastes said, *"Be not hasty in thy spirit to be angry: for anger resteth in the bosom of fools."* (Ecc. 7.9) In other words, if you keep anger and always display an angry spirit, you are a fool. That is not me speaking! That is the Word of God! No Saint of God should walk around with a mean and repulsive spirit. Our lives should be filled with the fruit of the Holy Spirit that are listed in Galatians 5.22-23: *"love, joy, peace, longsuffering, gentleness, goodness, faith, meekness, temperance: against such there is no law."*

Let me close this section by encouraging every believer to be a disciplined soldier for Jesus Christ. *Holiness* is God's way. Therefore, Holiness must be our lifestyle and standard for living. We, above all other people, must demonstrate the willingness to push towards the mark of spiritual excellence that God demands in the life of His children. Peter summed it up beautifully when he challenged the believers in the Lord and reminded them, *"But as he which hath called you is holy, so be ye holy in all manner of conversation: Because it is written, Be ye holy; for I am holy."* My friends, *our conversation* is the life that we live before God and the people in the world, *every day.* They believe what they see more than what they hear. I am a minister of the Gospel and the pastor of CCP. I often share with my congregation that the greatest message that I will ever preach is not in the church service on Sunday morning, but rather in the community where people from different backgrounds and cultures will read my life and discover my witness for Jesus Christ. What do they read in your life? *MAINTAIN YOUR SPIRITUAL DISCIPLINE!*

4. BE ALERT, STUDY AND KNOW WHO YOUR OPPONENT IS!

Every believer who intends to reach the status of a contender must know his or her opponent. There is no option. You must know who the opponent is! Paul said in verse 26, *"I therefore so run, not as uncertainly; so fight I, not as one that beateth the air:..."* This scripture suggests to us that there is a need to study and know your opponent prior to you engaging in the competition or battle. Paul said that he ran or competed with certainty, with full knowledge and a clear understanding of the opponent's capabilities. In other words, he knew exactly what he needed to do in order to win the competition and beat his challengers.

Many athletes failed to win the competition because they did not spend adequate time discovering the strengths and weaknesses of their opponent. Please note the point that I used the word *discovering* instead of noticing or acknowledging the capabilities of the opponent. Discover means to uncover, reveal and detect something that has been hidden or concealed. God has revealed to me that simply looking and observing the actions and

24

activities of the enemy is not enough. No legitimate opponent will permit anyone who poses a threat to their success to gain insights into their strengths or weaknesses via simple observations. As the old saying goes, "it is for me to know and for you to find out!" *You must dig to discover;* and digging is not easy! In fact, it is hard work! I will never forget the years that my Dad made my brother and I assist him in planting his vegetable garden in the springtime. Every year we dreaded the week prior to Good Friday because we knew that we would have to dig and cultivate a sizable portion of the back yard so that Dad could plant his garden vegetables on Good Friday. No matter how you sliced it or how big we grew physically, digging that garden was always hard work and nothing could make us like it. Even though we knew that we would enjoy the fruit of our labor when the greens, squash, cabbage and cucumbers grew; or the tomatoes, beets, okra and other vegetables blossomed; we still hated digging that garden because it was hard work! *Lookers are losers, but diggers are dedicated.* It takes dedication to study any thing. I did not say read, but study! That is why many Christians live defeated lives today, because they do not study the Bible, they only read it! The Lord told the Prophet Hosea, *"My people are destroyed for lack of knowledge:"* (Hos. 4.6) The lack of knowledge in this scripture literally means ignorance concerning the things of God. You must dig to discover the blessed benefits of God. We miss out on many of the things that God intends for us to enjoy because we do not know about them! Jesus said, *"seek, and ye shall find."* (Mat. 7.7) Seeking is a determined search with purpose. Before you seek, you must know what you are seeking or searching for.

Paul said, *"I therefore so run, not as uncertainly; so fight I, not as one that beateth the air:..."* Notice the choice selection of words that he used at the end of that scripture: *"so fight I, not as one that beateth the air:..."* Paul is informing the church that there must be an identifiable target to engage if you are going to score points in the competition. He says that he is not just swinging to be swinging! He is swinging and fighting to engage the enemy so that he can destroy him! Just in case you did not know, or have forgotten, *THE DEVIL IS OUR OPPONENT!* Contrary to popular belief, that person that gets under your skin at work and is always pressing against your last nerve is not your enemy. We often suffer defeat in ministry because we attempt to fight a spiritual enemy with physical methods. Paul reminded the Corinthian believers that our weapons and warfare are not based on worldly principles, but spiritual power! Paul said, *"For the weapons of our warfare are not carnal, but mighty through God,..."* In other words, our weapons are spiritual and are designed to engage and defeat spiritual foes. God supplies our weapons *"to the pulling down of strong holds; Casting down imaginations, and every high thing that exalteth itself against the knowledge of God, and bringing into captivity every thought to the obedience of Christ;"* (II Cor. 10. 3-5) We will discuss this point in more detail in a later chapter.

The Apostle Peter exhorted the Saints of God to *"Be sober, be vigilant; because your adversary the devil, as a roaring lion, walketh about, seeking whom he may devour:"* (I Pet. 5.8) In this verse, Peter is telling the church to stay alert and on guard so that they can stay alive! In other words, you cannot just run to be running! You must always be aware of your opponent! If you ever lose sight of your opponent, he will defeat you in competition and destroy you in battle. I will never forget the 1998 Belmont Stakes Horse Race because the Lord gave me this point while I watched that race. "Real Quiet" was the odds on favorite to win the race that year and become the first triple-crown winner in over twenty years. He lost sight of his opponent, "Victory Gallop", and lost at the wire by a nose! How awful that must have been. It made me sick looking at it on television. I could only imagine how the owners, the trainer and the jockey must have felt. However, I learned an important spiritual lesson from the Lord that will help me in my battle against the devil for the rest of my life: YOU MUST ALWAYS BE AWARE OF YOUR OPPONENT! "Real Quiet" lost the race because he did not know that "Victory Gallop" had come up on the outside and passed him before he could respond. That is what the devil is trying to do to you and me. He is literally walking and sneaking around in our life, meddling here and there, until he can seize an opportunity to launch an all out attack against us and devour us. *BE ALERT, STUDY AND KNOW WHO YOUR OPPONENT IS!*

5. TRIM THE FAT!

In other words, STRIP OFF THE EXCESS BAGGAGE! If you are going to be a successful contender in any sport or athletic event, you must be in tip-top condition. This section parallels the *"Train Hard"* section above. The result of good training is excellent conditioning. You cannot be fat and fit at the same time! I do not mean to be offensive, but it is true. In fact, you can be big and exceptionally strong without being fat. Leanness in athletics is usually associated with a high level of physical fitness. In most cases, the athletes who are in the greatest shape are the ones that have the lowest percent body fat. I mentioned earlier that I have a cousin that plays professional baseball for the Baltimore Orioles. He constantly watches what he eats and is always working out to increase his fitness level during the off-season as well as throughout the competitive baseball season. Alan only has about 8-10 % body fat and is constantly mindful that he maintains his weight at the recommended level throughout the year. He is amazing. I wish I could maintain 16% body fat anytime during the year without having to starve myself to death! Most people are conscious of their weight, especially women. This is good because it sets parameters and limits in our lives that govern and regulate what we will and will not do concerning our health and fitness regimen. Fitness does not just happen you must make it happen. I cannot stay a size 34 waist by wishing it. I must do something to get there and stay there. I will blow up like a balloon if I neglect my training discipline! It is shameful to see a person that is one size trying to wear or squeeze into clothes that are two sizes

27

smaller. The brain just has not accepted the fact that the body has increased in size and cannot wear the same clothes. Likewise, we must be equally mindful of the need to maintain our spiritual fitness level so that we can effectively compete for the Lord! The Lord does not want us to be fat in the Spirit. He wants us to be *"filled with the Spirit!"* (Eph. 5. 18)

Hebrews 12.1 says, *"Wherefore seeing we also are compassed about with so great a cloud of witnesses, LET US LAY ASIDE EVERY WEIGHT, AND THE SIN WHICH DOTH SO EASILY BESET US, and let us run with patience the race that is set before us,..."* This is the cornerstone scripture that I often use to encourage the Saints of God everywhere to perform *self-maintenance* in their personal life. The Hebrew writer was very familiar with the competitive sporting events, the national athletes and gladiators that competed or fought in the great forums, arenas and stadiums during that time. He observed the lifestyle and training strategies of the greatest heroes of that day and used them as examples to inspire the early Christians to employ the same diligence and discipline to achieve spiritual victory over the devil and the world. That one word keeps surfacing over and over again, *discipline.* You cannot make it and become a contender without discipline! A disciplined life in the Spirit of the Lord is a victorious life that is lived to the glory of God!

The Hebrew writer made a resounding cry when he said, *"we,* the believers in Jesus Christ, *are surrounded by a great cloud of witnesses..."* They are everywhere! These witnesses were the heroes of faith that were previously listed in Hebrews 11.1-40 and they are also the present day Saints who have influenced our faith and belief in God. They stripped themselves of all desires for worldly honor so that their witness for God would prevail against the most threatening foes, in the most deadly perils. They divested themselves of earthly glory and reverence to identify with the *faithful!* The scripture says, *"By faith Moses, when he was come to years, refused to be called the son of Pharaoh's daughter;..."* Moses was raised as the son of Pharaoh's daughter and was the heir to the throne of Egypt when he realized that he was truly a Hebrew. That realization moved him to defend one of his brethren when he was being punished and abused by an Egyptian. Moses counted up the cost of his action and determined that the Hebrew blood flowing through his veins was undeniably the essence of his purpose for living. Moses made a life-changing decision, *"Choosing rather to suffer affliction with the people of God, than to enjoy the pleasures of sin for a season; Esteeming the reproach of Christ greater riches than the treasures in Egypt: for he had respect unto the recompence of the reward."* (Hebrews 11:24-26) Moses made a choice to be identified with the oppressed people who worshipped and served the God of Israel and he rejected the Egyptian throne. He abandoned the pleasures of the palace of Egypt to become a shepherd in the austere Midian desert.

STRIPPING is God's strategy for the believer to maintain spiritual strength and experience His *dunamis power! Strip off, pull off, put off, take off* and *cast off* are common words that are directed by the Lord for all of the followers of Jesus Christ! You might say, "What does my Lord desire for me to take off?" I am glad that you asked! The Hebrew writer said, *"Let us lay aside EVERY WEIGHT, and THE SIN which doth so easily beset us,.....*" God wants us to drop the spiritual weights and the sin in our lives that will hinder us and prevent us from experiencing spiritual growth. Observe the difference between *weights* and *sin.*

Weights are not necessarily sinful things in our lives. However, they are things that hinder us from excelling or performing at our highest potential. The Greek word for *weight* in this scripture is *ogkos* (ong'-kos) and is described as being something that is a mass, a bulging load or a burden. More specifically, a spiritual weight is anything that is a hindrance in the lives of God's people and impedes their ability to *"grow in grace, and in the knowledge of our Lord and Saviour Jesus Christ."* (2 Pet 3:18) ESPN and sports in general can be serious weights in the brothers' lives that are sports fanatics like me. Our jobs can also become a huge weight for us. Television programs and special hobbies can be weights to the sisters. Our families and friends can be weights in all of our lives when they deter us from fulfilling our commitment to God and His church. Is there anyone or anything in your life that is hindering you or discouraging you from excelling in the Lord? (Husband, wife, children, boyfriend, girlfriend, best friend, career, social club, fraternal organization, hobby, possession, bad experience..... or *fear?*) Think about it for a moment. Spiritual weights bog you down, slow you down and sap all of your spiritual strength. We all know when we are not functioning at the proper level, naturally and spiritually. When our bodies are not functioning properly and we become sick, we all go to the doctor to receive treatment to get rid of the sickness or ailment. Likewise, the Lord is challenging us to inspect our spiritual loads, get rid of the weights in our life and make sure that what we are carrying will benefit us and glorify Him. *Weights* delay and degrade, but *Sin* is a different matter!

Sin does not impede or hinder; *it stops you* from moving forward in the Lord! What is sin? In essence, *Sin* is deliberate defiance, determined disobedience and faithless rebellion against the known will of God. The Greek word for sin in this scripture is *hamartia* (ham-ar-tee'-ah), which means an offence. It is the violation of the law of God in thought, word, and deed. *Sin* is actually a contradiction to the holiness and righteousness of God. The Apostle John said, *"Whosoever committeth sin transgresseth also the law: for sin is the transgression of the law."* (1 Jn 3:4) Ultimately, *Sin* separates us from God! The Prophet Isaiah told the Jewish nation of Israel, *"Behold, the LORD's hand is not shortened, that it cannot save; neither his ear heavy, that it cannot hear: But your iniquities have separated between you and your God, and your sins have hid his face from you, that he will not hear."* (Is. 59:1-2) The devastating effects of sin are visible throughout the world: in our government, in our own homes and communities, and in our church fellowships. Death and destruction are the result of sin! That is why the Hebrew author commanded the Saints of God to get rid of the sin in their life. *"Let us lay aside every weight, AND THE SIN which doth so easily beset us,…"* Sin defies the very authority of God as our Creator and places us under the judgement and wrath of God! In Colossians 3:5-10, the Apostle Paul encourages us to mortify or *"put to death your members which are on the earth: fornication, uncleanness, passion, evil desire, and covetousness, which is idolatry. Because of these things the wrath of God is coming upon the sons of disobedience, in which you yourselves once walked when you lived in them. But now YOU YOURSELVES are to PUT OFF all these: anger, wrath, malice, blasphemy, filthy language out of your mouth. Do not lie to one another, since YOU HAVE PUT OFF the old man with his deeds, and have PUT ON the new man who is renewed in knowledge according to the image of Him who created him."* (NKJ)

The Apostle Paul reminds us in his letter to the Ephesians that we have become new creations in the Lord and should spend our lives living in the victory of Jesus! Paul said, *"But you have not so learned Christ, if indeed you have heard Him and have been taught by Him, as the truth is in Jesus: that YOU PUT OFF, concerning your former conduct, the old man which grows corrupt according to the deceitful lusts, and be renewed in the spirit of your mind, that YOU PUT ON the new man which was created according to God, in true righteousness and holiness."* (Eph 4:20-24 NKJ) Romans 13:11-14 says, *"And do this, knowing the time, that now it is high time to awake out of sleep; for now our salvation is nearer than when we first believed. The night is far spent, the day is at hand. THEREFORE LET US CAST OFF THE WORKS OF DARKNESS, AND LET US PUT ON THE ARMOR OF LIGHT. LET US walk properly, as in the day, not in revelry and drunkenness, not in lewdness and lust, not in strife and envy. But PUT ON THE LORD JESUS CHRIST, and make no provision for the flesh, to fulfill its lusts."* (NKJ) Isn't God good? He does not intend for us to run around naked! When you take off your dirty clothes, nasty habits and sinful works of darkness, God enables you to put on the garments of His glory and His

31

righteousness! *Praise the name of the Lord!* Let's take it off and put them on to the glory of God!

Let me conclude this section by reiterating our key-point. *Stripping* is God's strategy for the believer to maintain spiritual strength and experience His *Dunamis power! Dunamis power* is that force or miraculous power that God gives to the believers, to enable them to perform mighty acts and accomplish the wonderful works of God! Many Christians sit back and wait for positive things to happen to them, or expect others to keep them in-line. We want the preacher to clean us up and keep us together. Today, God is telling every one of us to do *self-maintenance* by taking off all of the *weights* and *sin* that disgrace our witness and stand for Jesus Christ! The Lord told Moses and the children of Israel, *"CONSECRATE YOURSELVES therefore, and be holy, for I am the LORD your God. And you shall keep My statutes, and perform them: I am the LORD who sanctifies you."* (Lev. 20.7-8 NKJ) The Apostle Paul told the Corinthian church, *"Therefore, having these promises, beloved, LET US CLEANSE OURSELVES from all filthiness of the flesh and spirit, perfecting holiness in the fear of God."* (II Cor. 7.1 NKJ) *Weights* and *sin* put you in bondage and disqualify you from being a contender for Jesus Christ! Jesus died on Calvary so that we would be free from the burden and the bondage of sin. Because of the great price that Jesus paid for our freedom and deliverance from sin, Paul commands us to *"Stand fast therefore in the liberty by which Christ has made us free, and do not be entangled again with a yoke of bondage....You ran well. Who hindered you from obeying the truth?"* (Gal 5:1,7 NKJ)

The Lord is challenging you to *TRIM THE FAT* in your life. Take off the *weights* that hinder you and slow you down from running effectively for Jesus Christ. Get rid of the *sin* in your life before it destroys you! *The wages, the result and the compensation of SIN is still death!* I am praying that you will look inward and inspect your personal life to see if your commitment to Jesus is authentic or not. Do you really love Jesus more than anyone or anything else in this world? Paul commanded the Saints at Corinth to *"Examine yourselves, whether you be in the faith; prove your own selves."* (2 Cor 13:5) In other words, test yourself and check yourself to make sure that you are real! Please do not accept the devil's proposition and invitation to be a phony, Sunday morning Christian. If you have been one in the past, praise God that you do not have stay one, or be one in the future. Today is your opportunity to allow the Spirit of God to rule and govern your life. The psalmist said, *"Examine me, O LORD, and prove me; try my mind and my heart. For Your lovingkindness is before my eyes, and I have walked in Your truth."* (Ps 26:2-3 NKJ) The Lord does examine our hearts to see if there is anything that is competing with Him for the Lordship of our life. *TRIM THE FAT!*

6. HAVE FAITH IN GOD!

You cannot be a contender without faith! Hebrews 11:1 says *"Now faith is the substance of things hoped for, the evidence of things not seen."* I want you to know something else. *Faith is as funny as it is powerful!* It is true! I mean seriously. People laugh at faith! Why? Because genuine faith never makes common sense! In fact, *real faith is ridiculous!* I will never forget an experience I had with a prominent pastor of a successful ministry here in the Augusta, GA area. Our church (CCP) meets and holds our worship services and Bible studies in a high school cafeteria. We often say that we are meeting in the Glenn Hills High School cafeteria and we are serving up *Soul food!* One day I stopped by the school to make final coordination with the principle concerning our worship schedule and to make the first payment for our rental fee. While I waited to see the principle, the prominent pastor came into the office to pick up his daughter from school. We saw each other and began to share. He wondered what I was doing there, and thought maybe that my child attended the school too. I informed him that I was there to see the principle and take care of some final coordination for our church service. He was amazed when I told him that I had started my own ministry and that we met

33

at the school. He knew that I used to be the lead associate minister at another church. He and my former pastor are pretty good friends and I knew that he would contact him *to get the scoop on what Gainous was doing!* Therefore, he became suspect concerning my objective and could not hide it. That was strike one! He asked me what the name of my church fellowship was and I told him the *"Christian City of Praise!" (CCP).* I could read his thoughts, "another fly-by-night, uncalled for ministry and holy-roller church!" That was strike two! He then asked me, "when did you start the ministry and how many members do you have?" *I knew that my goose was cooked then!* I told him that I was just starting the ministry on the 27th of December 1998 (in two weeks) and I had four (4) members: my wife (Sharlotte), my daughter (Ebony), my mother-in-law (Ms. Bonnie M. Davison) and me. *That was the straw that broke the camel's back!* He looked as if he had seen a ghost! I stood there and began to smile. He tried to contain himself, but failed. He immediately dropped his eyes in disappointment and disbelief, shook his head, turned around and marched strait out of the principle's office without saying a word. *Not even goodbye!* I then started laughing because I knew what was going to be spread all over the city about me, and my *ridiculous ploy* to create a ministry! In fact, I am not sure he even stayed to pick up his daughter! (Just kidding) I finished my business there at the school, went home and told my wife what happened. We both had a hearty laugh over that incident. We now have over one hundred and twenty members and we are starting to grow like a little weed! Now some of you are laughing at the number of members that we currently have! That is all right! Keep on laughing! I know that the Lord has called Sharlotte and me to a tremendous ministry and we are enjoying the Lord while He is growing it Himself! *I praise God for faith to wait on Him and follow His word! He never makes a mistake!* Romans 8.31 says, *"What shall we then say to these things? IF GOD BE FOR US, WHO CAN BE AGAINST US?"* That is my position. *I am trusting in the Lord! WHO ARE YOU TRUSTING?*

I shared that story to say this. If you are not clear on your calling, and actively engaged in fulfilling it, you are a contestant. If you do not truly believe in the Lord and know His purpose for you in His service, you will always be a contestant. There is one common trait that you will find in all legitimate contenders, in any occupation, that is *faith!* *Contenders* are focused because they have faith! They are fearless because they have faith! They endure hardness and difficulties because they have faith! They overcome obstacles because they have faith! They actually believe that they will win before the event is started because they have faith! *"Now faith is the substance of things hoped for, the evidence of things not seen."* You have to win before you get on the field; before you take the test; before you engage in the battle! Winning is in your mind! We will discuss this point further in another chapter.

Many Christians are doomed because of unbelief. Today, most believers do not walk by faith. They walk by sight. If they can see it then they will believe it. Sense knowledge is not spiritual. It is natural. That is why the *Dunamis* power of God is not witnessed in most of our church fellowships. It is not that God is not moving any more. Testimonies across the continuum witness to the fact that He is still moving and demonstrating His awesome power before the world on a daily basis. It is because we do not have faith! If you cannot believe that the power of God will move in your life, it never will. Hebrews 11.6 tells us *"without faith it is impossible to please Him, for he who comes to God must believe that He is, and that He is a rewarder of those who diligently seek Him."* (NKJ) We are not seeing the demonstration of *His* power in our fellowships because we do not believe! Jesus said, *"A prophet is not without honor except in his own country, among his own relatives, and in his own house. Now He could do no mighty work there, except that He laid His hands on a few sick people and healed them. And He marveled because of their unbelief."* (Mark 6:4-6 NKJ) The scripture said that *Jesus marveled* because of their unbelief! The Greek word for *marveled*

35

in this verse is *thaumazo* (thou-mad'-zo); meaning to admire, have in admiration or wonder. In other words, their unbelief was so profound that Jesus, the King of Life and the Son of God, was amazed at the determined and rooted spirit of doubt that plagued the people of His own hometown. The Gospel of Matthew recorded that Jesus *"did not do many mighty works there because of their unbelief."* (Matt 13:58 NKJ) Let us take it a step further. How do you think God is looking at you, and the kind of faith that you demonstrate towards Him in your personal life? Is He *marveling* and *amazed* at your unbelief; or is He pleased with your faith in Him? Dear Saint of God, you must know and understand that *unbelief* stops the power and flow of God in your life. *Faith makes all of the difference in the world!*

Some of the most horrible words that a believer in Jesus Christ can use in his or her vocabulary are the words *"I cannot do..."* or *"I will not do..."* when it comes to working in the Kingdom of God. On the other hand, the same people that cannot do for the Lord can always find the strength and energy to do anything and everything that their bosses tell them to do at work! We cannot come to Sunday school, one day a week, on Sunday mornings because it is too early, and it starts at 9:00 am. Consequently, if we do show up, we are always late! However, we can make it to our secular jobs at 7:30 – 8:00 am, minimum five days a week, *on time,* and have to drive 15 – 60 miles *one way* to get there! We cannot make it out to mid-week Bible study, one day a week, on Wednesday evenings for 1-1/2 hours because we are too tired. However, we can work all day and stay late *without pay* if the boss needs us to do so. Isn't it amazing how our employers can influence us and energize us to do whatever needs to be done, whether we really feel like doing it or not? If they say it, we will do it! Subsequently, we can get home all tired and worn out from work, get the right phone call and immediately get instant energy to go out on the town with our friends, without a problem. Yet, we cannot respond to legitimate church requirements that arise from time to time without getting angry. Even more amazing is the fact that church parents can always seem to get their children to school and school events, *on time,* regardless of the time and place, but cannot find the time or energy to get their children to child evangelism sessions *at all!* I do not need to mention the other amazing things that we cannot do for God that we can do for man. (e.g. Study all night and read books to become more proficient at our jobs, or for enjoyment; teach formal classes to people we do not know; join secular auxiliaries and clubs; volunteer our services on weekends; participate in and become leaders in professional organizations; etc.) Oooh no, now you are feeling that I am stepping on toes. No, I am not intentionally stepping on anyone's toes. I am simply telling the truth. Remember Jesus said, *"the truth will make you free!"* The bottom line is that your actions speak louder than your words! You can do what you want to do, when you want to do it! That is the winning spirit! The power was prevalent in the early church because they believed in the word and the promises of God! They believed that God was with them to deliver them, to sustain them and heal their sicknesses and diseases! *Their faith made them powerful!*

Let me share another experience. When I was a senior in high school, my brother was a freshman in college and he decided to pledge a fraternity. Throughout his pledge period I would see him running around with his pledge brothers doing projects and community service events that I knew were very taxing. I would overhear him talking to one of his big brothers on the telephone and he would respond to every one of his big brother's statements by saying, "yes big brother, or no big brother." I thought this was ridiculous and I would start talking in the background to distract and interrupt my brother's conversation. I would say crazy things like, "Man, don't call that chump big brother! You do not have to listen to him! Who does he think he is? Do what you want to do! He does not control your life! I would not take that from anybody! Give me the phone, I will tell him where to go and how to get there! They must be crazy to think that somebody is going to bow down to them, just to be able to wear a silly T-shirt with some

37

funny looking Greek letters on it." I went on and on and on with my comments. Little did I know that a year later I would be pledging the same fraternity, with the same big brothers that I talked so horribly to on the phone. They did not forget what I had said throughout my brother's pledge period and they hit me like *a Texas tornado* when I showed up at the first pledge meeting. In fact, my own brother did not forget what I had said when he was pledging and he made sure that I remembered my words and ate every one of them! He hit me like a *Florida hurricane!* He terrorized me! Jesus said, *"For by your words you will be justified, and by your words you will be condemned."* (Matt 12:37 NKJ) My words condemned me! I could not have imagined all that my line brothers and I would have to go through to become members of the fraternity. Nevertheless, it was an extreme experience to say the least and I subjected myself to many uncomfortable things, just to get into the frat. What is my point? You can and will do just what you want to do, if your desire to achieve your goal is strong enough! The Apostle Paul said, *"I press toward the goal for the prize of the upward call of God in Christ Jesus."* (Phil 3:14 NKJ) Nothing can stop a determined contender for Jesus Christ! The spirit of the true contender says, *"I can do all things through Christ who strengthens me."* (Phil 4:13 NKJ)

You must believe that GOD is with you and will give you the victory! The story of David slaying Goliath in 1 Samuel chapter 17 is one of my favorite Bible stories. You must read it for yourself, if you have not read it before. It speaks to the confidence and faith that the Lord intends for all of His followers to possess. David was a small, ruddy looking shepherd boy who was anointed by the Prophet Samuel to be God's future king over the nation of Israel. In the story, David visited his brothers on the battlefield when King Saul and Israel were facing the Philistine Army and their great champion of Gath, Goliath the giant. Goliath intimidated the forces of Israel to the point that they feared him and would not fight against him. When David showed up and found his brothers, he asked them how the battle was going and then he heard Goliath challenge the whole army of Israel for any man among them to come out and fight him in a decisive battle to determine which nation would win the victory. Goliath's presence was so intimidating that the scripture said, *"And all the men of Israel, when they saw the man, fled from him and were dreadfully afraid."* Can you imagine that? One man caused an entire army to flee! However, David did not buy it and volunteered to fight the giant.

What made David different from the rest? *His faith in the Living God!* To hasten to my point, I want you to observe David's attitude concerning Goliath's challenge and threats against him. The scripture says, *"Now when the words which David spoke were heard, they reported them to Saul; and he sent for him. Then David said to Saul, 'Let no man's heart fail because of him; your servant will go and fight with this Philistine.' And Saul said to David, 'You are not able to go against this Philistine to fight with him; for you are a youth, and he a man of war from his youth.'"* Saul tried to discourage David from fighting Goliath because of the way he looked. People will tell you not to believe God and will try to discourage you from doing the very things that God has put in your spirit to do for Him. David is a picture of faith and confidence in God! Rather than allowing Saul's advice to discourage him, he shared with Saul some of the reasons why he was absolutely sure that he would defeat the giant. David said to Saul, *"Your servant used to keep his father's sheep, and when a lion or a bear came and took a lamb out of the flock, I went out after it and struck it, and delivered the lamb from its mouth; and when it arose against me, I caught it by its beard, and struck and killed it. Your servant has killed both lion and bear; and this uncircumcised Philistine will be like one of them, seeing he has defied the armies of the living God."* Moreover David said, *"The LORD, who delivered me from the paw of the lion and from the paw of the bear, He will deliver me from the hand of this Philistine."* Saul was amazed by his faith and said to David, *"Go, and the LORD be with you!"*

My dear friend, the Holy Spirit is telling me to tell you to *have faith in God!* It does not matter what you are facing in your personal life. God is able to give you the victory over it, *if you will believe!* Some of the giants that you have been facing in your life may have caused you to fear and not fight, and have turned you from being a contender to a contestant. There are all types of giants that stand up and defy our position in the Lord! They challenge your peace and security in your life. They may be trying to destroy your marriage right now, disrupt your relationships, kill your children, ruin your reputation and dissolve all of your hope. But today, the Lord commands you to *"Fear not, stand still, and see the salvation of the LORD, which he will show to you to day:... The LORD shall fight for you, and you shall hold your peace."* (Exod 14:13-14) In other words, as my associate minister so eloquently has stated, *"step back and watch God go to work!"*

Faith is the driving force of the Christian contender! Contenders take the field every time, regardless of the qualifications of their opponents. Christian contenders can be sure that they will win because of what they know about God! That is why David defeated Goliath, because of what he knew about God! Our experiences with God enable us to continue against the odds because we know that God gives us the victory! Roman 5:1-4 says, *"Therefore being justified by faith, we have peace with God through our Lord Jesus Christ: By whom also we have access by faith into this grace wherein we stand, and rejoice in hope of the glory of God. And not only so, but we glory in tribulations also: knowing that tribulation worketh patience; and patience, experience; and experience, hope:"* You may have lost some battles, but you cannot lose the war! The scripture said, *"And when the Philistine looked about and saw David, he disdained him* [despised him]*; for he was only a youth, ruddy and good-looking."* Goliath was looking outward, but David's *faith* was internal. Goliath thought that his immense size, his natural strength and his intimidating stare were enough to defeat Israel's warrior, but he was wrong! He was not facing David. He was facing *the Faith of*

David! David said to the Philistine, *"You come to me with a sword, with a spear, and with a javelin. But I come to you in the name of the LORD of hosts, the God of the armies of Israel, whom you have defied. This day the LORD will deliver you into my hand, and I will strike you and take your head from you. And this day I will give the carcasses of the camp of the Philistines to the birds of the air and the wild beasts of the earth, that all the earth may know that there is a God in Israel. Then all this assembly shall know that the LORD does not save with sword and spear; for the battle is the LORD'S, and He will give you into our hands."* David made this declaration by faith, *before the battle was fought,* and then he went forward and destroyed Goliath the giant with a single stone from his sling! That is the result of a *pure and living faith!*

My dear friend, please allow me close this section with these words of encouragement. Jesus said, *"If you have faith as a mustard seed, you will say to this mountain, 'Move from here to there,' and it will move; and nothing will be impossible for you."* (Matt 17:20 NKJ) The Lord also said, *"If you have faith as a mustard seed, you can say to this mulberry tree, 'Be pulled up by the roots and be planted in the sea,' and it would obey you."* (Luke 17:6 NKJ) *Fear* is the opposite of *faith. Fear* causes the believer to fall to the level of a contestant. Contenders are filled with *faith* and *Dunamis power!* Isaiah 54.17 says, *"No weapon formed against you shall prosper, and every tongue which rises against you in judgment you shall condemn. This is the heritage of the servants of the LORD, and their righteousness is from Me, says the LORD."* Therefore, *HAVE FAITH IN GOD!*

7. FINISH STRONG!

Finally, if you are going to be a legitimate contender for Jesus Christ, *YOU MUST TO BE A STRONG FINISHER!* A *finisher* is a person who completes a project. The Greek word for finisher is teleiotes (tel-i-o-tace') and it refers to completing or bringing to an end or finish. The word is applied to Jesus Christ in

41

Hebrews 12:2 and describes Him as being the completer and consummater of our *faith* in God. The Hebrew writer declares that Jesus is in fact *"the author and finisher of our faith."* When you think about it, finishing is a part of our daily life. All of us have been taught to finish diverse things since the moment we were born. When we were wee babies and could not clean ourselves or even say a word, our mothers would ask us if we had finished *our business,* then they would clean us up. As we grew older and were able to eat food, our mothers asked us if we had finished our meal. Our fathers asked us if we had finished our chores. I know that my brother and I had to finish our work around the house before we could go out and play with our friends. Our parents often asked us if we had finished our homework and church work before they would permit us to participate in other leisure activities. Finishing is a part of life. Today as adults and work professionals, our employers and bosses assign us projects and tasks to complete on our jobs that we must finish in order to maintain a good standing with them and keep our jobs. So it should not be unnatural for any of us to accept and understand the fact that *finishing* is also a requirement in the Lord's service.

It is not good enough to start and not finish. We have many *contestants* around the church, but only a few *real contenders!* A contestant will volunteer to fulfill a responsibility within the church ministry and will work in that capacity until it becomes burdensome or an inconvenience. When that happens, and they become challenged in the work, they will abandon ship and let that part of the ministry fail. Have you made a commitment to fulfill or support a particular ministry in your local church fellowship? Have you been faithful in your efforts to do your part to ensure that it prospers and blesses the members of your church, or have your started and quit? *Contestants* are like the hireling that Jesus described in ST John 10:11-13. Jesus said, *"I am the good shepherd. The good shepherd gives His life for the sheep. But a hireling, he who is not the shepherd, one who does not own the sheep, sees the wolf coming and leaves the sheep and flees; and the wolf catches the sheep and scatters them. The hireling flees because he is a hireling and does not care about the sheep."* (NKJ) A contestant is just like a hireling in the church, and will not finish anything that they are responsible for if it does not fall in line with his or her personal agenda and comfort level. *A contender* will finish whatever he or she is involved in, no matter what it takes, regardless of what he or she faces, despite how hard the challenges may be, or how hot the battles may get. *He or she will finish the course!*

I attended General Dwight D. Eisenhower Senior High School in Lawton, OK and was a member on the school's track team. I ran third leg on the varsity 440-yard, 880-yard, sprint-medley and mile-relay teams all three years that I attended high school. I remember the relay tryouts that our track coach (Coach Bowman) made us run to determine the four members of the different relay teams. He would line up the top eight runners and make us compete against each other in the 100-yard, 220-yard and 440-yard dashes. (I know that I am telling my age now because they no longer run these races in yards, they run them in meters.) Nevertheless, I remember that the anchor runner was always the fastest person on the relay team and the strongest finisher. If you have the right anchor runner, you can win the race even if he or she gets the baton in last place. Their strength, power and exceptional speed enable them to pull in the other runners who may be ahead of them in the race. My senior year, we had the best anchor runner and the fastest sprinter in the state of Oklahoma on our team. His name is Henry Williams. Henry could *fly!* He was the state champion in the 100 and 220-yard dashes. We had a quick starter (Don McGee), two good intermediate legs (Terry Gamble and yours truly) and a great anchor runner (Henry). It took all of us to win the relay race, but Henry was our guarantee that if we just ran our leg with any measure of success we would always win the race. Why? Because Henry was the greatest finisher in the state! Consequently, we have a lot of *quick starters* and *good intermediate racers* in the church, but only a few worthy *anchor runners!* The Lord needs somebody that will start strong, run strong and finish strong! God needs somebody that will get in, stay in and finish the race for Jesus Christ! *Be a contender, not just a contestant!*

Completion is the objective and goal of the believer. The bottom line is this, if you cannot finish, whatever it is, you should never start. Jesus used several parables to communicate this point to His disciples. One in particular was the parable of the tower builder in Luke 14:28-30. Jesus said, *"For which of you, intending to build a tower, does not sit down first and count the cost, whether he has enough to finish it lest, after he has laid the foundation, and is not able to finish, all who see it begin to mock him, saying, 'This man began to build and was not able to finish.'"* (NKJ) This lets me know that finishing is important to God! Jesus spoke this same sentiment to His disciples in ST John 4:34 when He said, *"My meat is to do the will of him that sent me, AND TO FINISH HIS WORK."* Finishing is important to God! If you are going to be a legitimate contender for Jesus Christ, you have to finish the race, finish the fight and finish the work of God!

Let us consider the Boston Marathon and the thousands of people who run in that great race. Of all the statistics that are available to review on that race, the ones that are the most significant to me are the number of competitors that entered the race, the number of competitors that started the race and the number of competitors that actually finished the race. I surfed the Internet and ran across some of these statistics at the Boston Marathon web site. The following table and race summary is provided for your review and information. The race participant data outlines the number of athletes in each category that participated in the race. There were 17,813 entrants in the runners' category that signed up for the race. Of those runners, there were 1,686 runners that did not start the race and only 15,646 runners actually finished the race. That means 481 runners who started the race quit or fell out of the race because of various reasons. *I will not knock them because I would have fallen out too, and I am sure*

I would have fallen out first! However, if you review the different categories of participants, the Hand-cycle category athletes were the only group of participants that had every person that started the race actually finish the race.

Boston Marathon 2000 Participant Data

	Entrants	Starters	Finishers
Runners	17, 813	16, 127	15, 646
Wheelchairs	64	53	49
Hand-cycles	13	11	11
Mobility Impaired (10:00 a.m. Start)	7	7	4
Mobility Impaired (Noontime Start)	5	5	4
Visually Impaired	19	19	18

Boston Marathon 2000 Race Summary

Boston Marathon 2000™ proved worthy of its advanced billing as the 104th running of the world's oldest annually contested marathon resulted in one of the most compelling and entertaining all-around performances in event history.

The first champion to be crowned was Franz Nietlispach, of Switzerland, who obliterated a loaded men's wheelchair division field to claim his fourth consecutive title and fifth overall. In the women's wheelchair race, Jean Driscoll, of Illinois, dethroned three-time champion Louise Sauvage, of Australia, and registered an unprecedented eighth Boston Marathon title.

For the first time in the history of the men's race, three competitors rounded the final turn together onto Boylston Street, where Kenyan Elijah Lagat unleashed a surprising kick to overhaul compatriot Moses Tanui and Ethiopian Gezahenge Abera. Lagat and Abera were credited with an identical finishing time (2:09:47), marking the closest finish in race history, while two-time former champion Tanui finished three seconds back (2:09:50), to mark the closest finish between the first three.

Many expected the women's open race to conclude with Ethiopia's Fatuma Roba becoming the first four-time champion in event history. Hence, it came as no surprise when she pulled away during the hills. However, Kenyan Catherine Ndereba pulled even on the final summit, and, after matching strides along Beacon Street, began to pull away on Commonwealth Avenue. While Ndereba sprinted to victory on Boylston Street (2:26:11), Irina Bogacheva, of Kyrgyzstan, passed the fading Roba at the line, where the duo registered an identical time (2:26:27). Like the men's race, it marked the closest finish between first and second (16 seconds) and first and third (also 16 seconds).

In the masters division, Kenyan Joshua Kipkemboi, who was runner-up a year ago, dethroned two-time defending champion Andrey Kuznetsov, of Russia, while Denmark's Gitte Karlshoj posted a winning time of 2:35:11, which stands as the sixth fastest in division history.

The top Americans on the day were Jamie Hibell, of Pennsylvania (24th; in 2:22:52), and masters runner Maria Trujillo de Rios, of California (18th; 2:42:24).

The 2000 Boston Marathon Race Summary also informs us that the event was an exceptional race that had several categories of entrants finishing within seconds of the winners.

Finishing is a part of winning! You cannot win any competition unless you finish the requirements. The Ephesian elders knew that the Apostle Paul's life was endangered if he traveled to Jerusalem to attend the Feast of Pentecost and they tried to discourage him from doing so. Nevertheless, when they approached him, Paul said to them: *"You know, from the first day that I came to Asia, in what manner I always lived among you, serving the Lord with all humility, with many tears and trials which happened to me by the plotting of the Jews; how I kept back nothing that was helpful, but proclaimed it to you, and taught you publicly and from house to house, testifying to Jews, and also to Greeks, repentance toward God and faith toward our Lord Jesus Christ. And see, now I go bound in the spirit to Jerusalem, not knowing the things that will happen to me there, except that the Holy Spirit testifies in every city, saying that chains and tribulations await me. BUT NONE OF THESE THINGS MOVE ME; nor do I count my life dear to myself, SO THAT I MAY*

46

FINISH MY RACE WITH JOY, AND THE MINISTRY WHICH I RECEIVED FROM THE LORD JESUS, to testify to the gospel of the grace of God." (Acts 20:18-24 NKJ) This passage of scripture confirms the fact that completion is required in the Lord's service! If you start in the race, you must finish.

Let me conclude this section with these thoughts. If you do not finish the work that the Lord has assigned for you to do in His service, you will answer to Him. The Holy Spirit is telling you and leading you do something significant in ministry at your local church fellowship, *but you have not obeyed.* You are dissatisfied with where your are in the Lord and realize that your life has much more value to God than what Satan has convinced you to believe and accept. *Right now,* the Holy Spirit is prompting you to answer God's call and fulfill your purpose within the body of Jesus Christ. You must respond by faith! Get off the devil's sideline and get onto the playing field for the Lord! The devil will tell you that it is too late and everybody will be suspect if you volunteer to support an auxiliary in the church again. They may be suspect because of your past history and unfaithfulness. However, do not let the feelings of others stop your from obeying the voice of the Lord. Remember what we shared before from 1 Samuel 15:22, *"And Samuel said, Hath the LORD as great delight in burnt offerings and sacrifices, as in obeying the voice of the LORD? Behold, TO OBEY IS BETTER THAN SACRIFICE, and to hearken than the fat of rams."* Saul's decision to disobey the voice of God cost him the throne of Israel and his relationship with the Lord.

You must be faithful in all of your commitments with the Lord. *Faithfulness maintains our fellowship with God!* The Apostle Paul told the Philippian church that he thanked God for their faithfulness and fellowship in the gospel of Jesus Christ. They demonstrated their love for the Lord and other Christians from the first day they were born into the kingdom of God. Paul said that he was *"confident of this very thing, that He who has begun a good work in you will complete it until the day of Jesus Christ."* (Phil 1:3-6 NKJ) We all need to know and understand this point. God is not satisfied with starting a work in your life. *He wants to complete the work in you until the day of Jesus Christ!* Therefore, the Lord intends to use our whole life to glorify His name continually. The only way that will happen is if you are in a usable condition. The Lord cannot flow through your life when it is polluted by sin. *Remember our discussion about weights and sin in our previous section "TRIM THE FAT!"* Sin will stop you in your tracks! The Psalmist said in Psalms 66:18, *"If I regard iniquity in my heart, the Lord will not hear me."* You must be clean within your heart for the Lord to use you. You notice that I did not say *perfect,* because none of us will reach perfection until the Lord comes back again. However, God's definition of perfection in the believers' life is having the right attitude towards God and placing *His will* as the priority and paramount thing in your life. If you are ever going to finish the work and calling of God that He has given you to accomplish, you must allow the God to sit on the throne of your life and truly honor Him as Lord.

    Finally, you must finish the race to receive the prize! Nobody will win without finishing! Some of our courses will be longer than others. Some will take us through more dangers and disappointments than we can imagine. Some of our courses will cause us to run alone, without the benefit of other runners to encourage us to continue in the race. Therefore, *finishing* must be an internal drive that motivates every believer to press on to the end by faith. Jesus said in ST Matthew 10:22, *"And you will be hated by all for My name's sake. BUT HE WHO ENDURES TO THE END WILL BE SAVED."* (NKJ) Jesus also warned us to be courageous while we run the Christian race. He told the Apostle John to write to the angel of the church in Smyrna saying, *"Do not fear any of those things which you are about to suffer. Indeed, the devil is about to throw some of you into prison, that you may be tested, and you will have tribulation ten days. Be faithful until death, and I will give you the crown of life."* (Rev 2:10 NKJ)

    Eternal Life is the finish line for all believers! Every other event and competition that we enter in this life begins and ends in this life, except our salvation and Christian calling. The Lord Jesus saves by His grace and commissions us by His Holy Spirit to enter the Christian race for God. Nobody in this world started you and nobody in this world can set your finish line when it comes to the eternal things of God. Only Jesus can establish the endpoint in our Christian race. The Hebrew writer declares that Jesus is the supreme runner that we should look to for our encouragement and example to follow. I am encouraged to continue to the end because of what Jesus has done for all of us. Hebrews 12:1-4 says, *"Therefore we also, since we are surrounded by so great a cloud of witnesses, let us lay aside every weight, and the sin which so easily ensnares us, and let us run with endurance the race that is set before us, LOOKING UNTO JESUS, THE AUTHOR AND FINISHER OF OUR FAITH, who for the joy that was set before Him endured the cross, despising the shame, and has sat down at the right hand of the throne of God. For consider Him who endured such hostility from sinners against Himself, lest you become weary and discouraged in your souls. You have not yet resisted to bloodshed, striving against sin."* (NKJ)

Yes, my dear friend, we are running and pressing towards an eternity with Jesus Christ our Lord! Jesus is at the finish line cheering and encouraging us to *finish strong!* Paul summed it up perfectly when he said, *"For I am now ready to be offered, and the time of my departure is at hand. I HAVE FOUGHT A GOOD FIGHT, I HAVE FINISHED MY COURSE, I HAVE KEPT THE FAITH: Henceforth there is laid up for me a crown of righteousness, which the Lord, the righteous judge, shall give me at that day: and not to me only, but unto all them also that love his appearing."* (2 Tim 4:6-8) (KJV) We all will finish our race when we close our eyes in death on this side and wake up in eternity to be with Jesus forever! Will you see the Lord's face in peace? *FINISH STRONG!*

Chapter III

NO COMPROMISE

"And be not conformed to this world..." (Rom 12:2)

If you are ever going to please God and be a legitimate contender for Jesus Christ, you must be Holy. My dear friend, questionable Christian character is destroying the witness of the body of Christ throughout our nation today. I use the term *nation* because America is the most dominant Christian-Faith country in the world. We are failing to uphold the standard of Holiness in our nation. You may be asking yourself, *"What is holiness?"* Let me share some thoughts and then give you a basic definition. First of all, let me share what *holiness is not! Holiness is not* a jump and a shout, or any action that is motivated by natural emotions. *Holiness is not* flipping over church pews, running up and down the isle and knocking people over in worship services. Contrary to some popular belief, *holiness is not* speaking in tongues, a pious look or a long list of rules and regulations dictating what you can and cannot do in your life. *Holiness is a lifestyle!* That is what God wants you and me to understand. *__Holiness is a lifestyle!__*

By definition, *holiness* is moral and ethical wholeness or perfection. It is freedom from moral evil. It may also be rendered *"sanctification"* or *"godliness."* Therefore, the word holy denotes that which is *"sanctified"* or *"set apart"* for divine service. More specifically, *holiness* is one of the inherent attributes of God. *What is an attribute?* An attribute is an intrinsic or innate characteristic of a person or being. For instance, some people are naturally funny and humorous, and everyone likes to be around them. Great athletes are naturally gifted to play certain sports at an exceptional level. Some women can eat anything they want, never exercise and still look great because they are naturally beautiful and were

51

born with the *right stuff!* They often are the envy of others too! Many of us were born with the physical, mental and emotional attributes of our parents! You would be surprised to discover the many different types of attributes that we receive from our parents. People often tell me that I look just like my Daddy. One young man in our church fellowship *walks* exactly like his father! A friend of mine even shared that his little three year-old son will not wear any *underwear* unless they look exactly like the ones he wears! Can you believe that? In the same manner, *Holiness* is associated with the *natural* attributes of God. *God is naturally holy!* While we cannot describe God in a comprehensive way, we can learn about Him by examining *His attributes* as revealed in the Bible. Isaiah 6:1-8 clearly describes and presents one of the most vivid and comprehensive views of God in the bible. The true and living God is separated from and exalted above all other things! *He is Holy and the whole earth is filled with His glory! Hallelujah!*

Holiness also refers to God's *moral excellence* and is one of the essential elements of God's nature that is required of His people. Because God is holy, He demands holiness in His own children. The Apostle Peter preached this point and said, *"but as He who called you is holy, you also be holy in all your conduct, because it is written, 'Be holy, for I am holy.'"* (1 Pet 1:15-16 NKJ) The good news is found in the fact that *what God demands, He supplies! Praise the Lord!* In fact, the very essence of the living God is imparted to His children through the gift of the Holy Spirit. Every believer in Jesus Christ has the Holy Spirit and was born into the family of God by the Spirit of Jesus Christ! Romans 8.9 says *"Now if any man have not the Spirit of Christ, he is none of His."* Therefore, *holiness* is God's gift that we receive by faith through His Son. *Jesus Christ was the very personification of God's divine holiness!*

Let me present another angle. Many people live twisted lives. They declare themselves to be lovers of God, but live a lifestyle that speaks another language. There is no consistency in

52

their walk. My dear friend, what you say does not determine who you are. What you do determines who you are in the Lord! A lot of people can talk a good game. Just like me! I can talk a lot of noise off the basketball court, but when I get on the court I must be able to back my talk up with some serious B-ball skills. That is what God is saying to the church today. *It is not so much what you say, as much as it is what you do.* You can say that you are on fire for the Lord, but what you do says that you are as cold as ice. You can say that you love the Lord, but what you do speaks another word. Jesus reproved the scribes and Pharisees concerning their religious piety and self-made traditions when he repeated the words of the Prophet Isaiah, *"These people draw near to Me with their mouth, and honor Me with their lips, but their heart is far from Me. And in vain they worship Me, teaching as doctrines the commandments of men."* (Matt 15:8-9 NKJ) The Lord is telling us that the lifestyle of holiness is a consistent walk with God, *according to His divine word.* It is a holy lifestyle, whether it is on Sunday morning or any other day in the week! It is even holy on Friday and Saturday nights when everybody else is out jumping at the clubs. God is calling for *"True Holiness"* in the lifestyle of His children. The Apostle Paul encouraged the believers in Ephesus to *"put on the new man, which after God is created in righteousness and true holiness."* (Eph 4:24) The mention of the term *true holiness* in the scripture suggests that there is a false sense or demonstration of holiness on display in the world. Our Lord is telling us that we must be holy and righteous to be an effective witness for Jesus Christ. ***Righteousness is embedded in God's holiness!*** Contenders do not have to talk a big game. They go out everyday and show that they have a big game for Jesus Christ! That is why James said, *"But someone will say, 'You have faith, and I have works.' Show me your faith without your works, and I WILL SHOW YOU MY FAITH BY MY WORKS. For as the body without the spirit is dead, so faith without works is dead also."* (James 2:18,26 NKJ) *Christian contenders* give it all *everyday,* and lay everything out on the line, *every time* they take the *spiritual* battlefield or court for the Lord! *They show their faith by their works! DO YOU?*

Now that we have broken the ice on the essence of *holiness,* lets focus on the second part of our primary scripture that supports this chapter, *"AND BE NOT CONFORMED TO THIS WORLD..."* The thought that I want to share with you in this chapter is *"NO COMPROMISE!"* That is what the Lord is telling the church today, *"NO COMPROMISE!"* You may be asking yourself, *"What does holiness have to do with 'NO COMPROMISE?'"* EVERYTHING! *Compromise is a direct result of failing to uphold the standard of holiness in some area of your life! Compromise is a contradiction to holiness!*

We compromise many things, to include our position and fellowship with God. By definition, to compromise is to give in, surrender and make amends so that two parties can basically come to an agreement. In other words, to compromise is to bargain, negotiate and make concessions in order to settle a difference of opinion. Ultimately, a compromise is a concession to something that is harmful or depreciative in your life. *WHEN YOU COMPROMISE YOU LOSE!* That is what God is communicating to us today. Do not compromise or bargain with the devil because when you do, *you are going to lose EVERY TIME!* The goal and objective of the devil is to get you to compromise your spiritual integrity with God. In doing so, you discredit your witness for Jesus Christ. The devil specializes in making deals that will destroy your life. Satan is trying to make a deal *with you* today. He is trying to strike a deal *with you,* to convince *you* that a carnal lifestyle and mediocrity in ministry are acceptable to God. Nevertheless, I want you to know and understand that God says, "NO COMPROMISE!" God does not desire or accept mediocrity in His people. *It is all or nothing and everything is on the line, EVERY DAY!* Jesus said that the first and great commandment that is written in scripture is, *"Hear, O Israel, the Lord our God is one Lord. And thou shalt love the Lord thy God with all thy heart, with all thy soul, and with all thy mind and with all thy strength. This is the first and the great commandment."* Now what is that telling us? *It is all or nothing with God and He is not settling for less!* He wants everything! He wants your whole being, your whole life and everything that you are. He wants the total and absolute surrender of all you are to Him! In other words, *the Lord wants YOU!*

There are three key points that I want to share with you in this chapter. First of all, *God wants to be in complete control of your life.* God is not happy unless He is controlling your life. You may please other people, but if you are not pleasing God, your life is out of order. Sister Sally, Brother Bob, your pastor or any other person may hold you in very high esteem based upon their personal desires or values, and this is good. However, *what really matters is where you stand with the Lord!* Many of us are seeking our own personal desires and objectives that are against the will of God. Jesus cannot help Himself to our lives unless we are *totally abandoned* and sold-out to Him. Now total abandonment means that God is in complete control of your life. Our statement to God from our heart should be, *"Help yourself Lord and have your way in my life!"* You cannot say those words unless you are totally sold-out to Jesus Christ. *You must yield to God on every point to become a Christian Contender!* Proverbs 3:5-6 says, *"Trust in the LORD with all thine heart; and lean not unto thine own understanding. IN ALL THY WAYS ACKNOWLEDGE HIM, and he shall direct thy paths."* You must allow God to have the right-of-way and the green light in every area of your life. When we travel down the road in our cities and suburbs, whoever has the green light has the right-of-way. The yellow light gives us caution and a warning that the light is about to change from green to red. The red light tells us that we must stop and wait our turn because someone else has the right of way. If we would do an assessment of who is leading our lives, many of us will discover that we have the *green light* in our lives. We are telling ourselves to go forward and do what we want to do. We are putting a *yellow light* on the church and *we are giving God a red light!* However, today, God is saying, *"I want to have the green light and the right-of-way in your life!"* *Praise His Wonderful Name!* God is so good. Even when we do not obey Him, or praise Him for His goodness, or do not do the things that we know He wants us to do, *He still loves us and is merciful towards us!* I do not know about you, but if justice were done in my life, I would have been dead a long time ago! If God had given me what I deserved, I would not be here today. *I praise God for His mercy!*

Do you ever really think about your life and all of the things that *could have gone wrong* when you were living in sin and walking in the desires of your flesh? Have you ever really sat down and counted the number of *close calls* you had when you were wrapped up in a sinful lifestyle? I often reflect back and look over my old life that I lived without Jesus Christ as my Lord and Savior. When I do so, I always feel the need to lift up my hands to God in great appreciation and *I thank God for His mercy! Hallelujah!* The psalmist said, *"Oh, give thanks to the LORD, for He is good! For His mercy endures forever."* (Ps 107:1 NKJ) *God's mercy is everlasting!*

Let me digress for a moment and share a short spiritual lesson. Do you know the difference between *grace* and *mercy*? *Grace* is unmerited or unearned favor. *Grace* is receiving what you do not deserve. It is something that is given to you by faith, without a demand for compensation, or act of labor. An example of *grace* is someone walking up to you and saying here, my brother or sister, receive this gift from me and enjoy it. *The giver does not even have to be a Christian and you do not have to like the gift!* It still qualifies as *grace.* **Divine Grace** *is an unearned gift of God and is a loving demonstration of His unmerited favor toward us!* You cannot earn it or pay it back. The Apostle Paul reminded the Ephesian church that their salvation was achieved only through the *grace of God.* Ephesians 2. 8-9 says, *"For by grace you have been saved through faith, and that not of yourselves; it is the gift of God, not of works, lest anyone should boast."*

56

Mercy, on the other hand, is someone withholding from us a right penalty that we deserve to receive for an offense that we have committed. A good example that comes to mind for me is a traffic cop giving or issuing you a *warning* rather than a real traffic ticket for speeding and breaking the law. *Mercy* always focuses on redemption and a type of deliverance from a burden or legitimate debt. Again, anyone can extend mercy to another without a limit. *Divine Mercy* is the aspect of God's love that causes Him to forgive the sinner who has committed offenses against the holiness and righteousness of God. That includes the many times in the past that we did things that we knew were wrong, and today when we commit acts that we know are sinful that can ruin our lives. Some of us have had to live for days, weeks and months wondering whether one particular sinful act that we committed would destroy our life. However, God, by His *great mercy,* withheld from us what we deserved to receive and prevented the tragic outcome that should have happened! *Thank God for His mercy!*

Divine Mercy is also that aspect of God's love that causes Him to help the miserable. Miserable, meaning those who are distressed and anguished because of circumstances beyond their control. We see this aspect of mercy especially in the life of our Lord Jesus. He healed blind men (Matt. 9:27-31; 20:29-34) and lepers (Luke 17:11-19), and even raised Lazarus from the dead as an act of *divine mercy* that was shown towards his sisters, Mary and Martha (John 11. 1-45). These acts of mercy grew out of his attitude of compassion and love for humanity. In essence, *Divine Mercy* is the deliverance God gives to people who are helpless and hopelessly guilty of sin, and to those who need of a divine blessing that will bring relief in their life. *I thank God for His mercy!* My dear friend, do you truly thank God for *His mercy?* How many times have you compromised with the devil and committed sinful acts that you know contradicted God's righteousness, but God was merciful to you? *O thank God for His mercy!* I praise the Lord that God did not give me what I deserved when Kenny Gainous

57

was living according to the sinful desires of his flesh. I could have died in my sins and gone strait to hell, but *thank God for His Mercy! HALLELUJAH!*

"NO COMPROMISE!" That is what God is telling all of the contenders for Jesus Christ today. *Do not compromise with the devil because you will lose every time!* You cannot say, *"Lord, have your way in my life,"* unless you are totally sold-out to Jesus! That is what the scripture is saying to us today, *"AND BE NOT CONFORMED TO THIS WORLD..."* In other words, do not give in to the world; do not compromise with the world; and *do not negotiate with the devil!* Peter shared some vital information to us in 1 Peter 5.7 to let us know why we should not play with the devil. He warned the believers and told them to, *"Be sober [be alert], be vigilant [be on your guard], because your adversary, the devil, [that means he is your enemy] walks about like a roaring lion, seeking whom he may devour."* The devil is not your ally. He is your enemy! For anybody that has ever been in the Army, we train to kill the enemy because the enemy is training to kill us! Peter said, the devil is going about *"as a roaring lion [walking up and down] seeking whom he may devour."* Peter went on to say, *"whom resist steadfast in faith."* James said, *"Submit yourselves therefore to God. Resist the devil, and he will flee from you."* (James 4:7) So, what is the Lord telling us? *God wants to be in complete control of your life!* **[POINT #1]**

Now the second point I need to share with you concerning "NO COMPROMISE" is this: *compromising with the devil and sin is dangerous and costly.* Playing around in sin is dangerous, can get you killed and cause you to lose everything! You may be asking yourself, "How is that?" I am glad you asked! Let us consider the life of Solomon. Remember when he was a child and became the king of Israel at a very young age? During that time, Solomon sought the Lord for wisdom above all other worldly riches and natural desires. Consequently, the Lord blessed Solomon beyond measure and gave him wisdom, power, wealth and riches! God gave him all of these wonderful blessings because his heart was set towards the Lord. The Bible says, *"Delight yourself also in the LORD, and He shall give you the desires of your heart. Commit your way to the LORD, trust also in Him, and He shall bring it to pass."* (Ps. 37.4-5 NKJ) Have you ever gotten what you wanted from the Lord? If you delight yourself in the Lord, He will give you some of the nice things that you desire, in righteousness. *God wants you to be happy! God wants you to be successful!* The Bible says in III John 2, *"Beloved, I wish above all things that you may prosper and be in health, even as you soul prospers."* God wants you to do well and be well in this world!

   Compromise is dangerous because it is the first step towards you becoming disobedient to God. Everything was well with Solomon, so long as he followed and obeyed the Lord. His fellowship with the Lord diminished when he started marrying and relating to the strange people in the land that God told him not to mingle nor associate with. Likewise, the Lord is telling us to watch and beware whom we set our association with in this world. Solomon disobeyed the commandment of God and began having sinful relationships with strange women and concubines from foreign nations. He married many of them and brought them into his kingdom for sinful pleasures. These women did not worship the true and living God, but idols and strange images from their sinful cultures. Eventually Solomon started participating in these idolatrous acts of pagan worship. That sin of idolatry became the downfall of his kingdom. *What is that telling us today?* When you compromise with the devil *you lose every time!* Just because everyone else is doing it does not mean that it is right for you. The Apostle Paul told the Corinthians believers who were living in the midst of a sinful culture, *"All things are lawful for me, but not all things are helpful; all things are lawful for me, but not all things edify."* (1 Cor 10:23 NKJ) If you are twenty-one years of age, there are places you can go that you cannot go if you were eighteen or nineteen. You can go to the juke joints and the strip joints. It is lawful and legal, *but is it pleasing to God?* That is the bottom line. *Is your involvement in anything that you do compromising your*

59

witness for Jesus Christ? That is the question that you must answer in your personal life.

I share with the members of our congregation that I do not get into the business of telling you what you can or cannot do. We outline this point in our CCP New Members Orientation Handbook that we give to the people who join our church fellowship. It is the Holy Spirit's responsibility to let you know what is acceptable and unacceptable to God. However, you can bet, if you do not find it supported by the Holy Scripture, it is not acceptable to God! Brother Kenny is not going to tell you that you do not need to go here nor there. I trust that through preaching and teaching the Word of God, under the anointing power of the Holy Spirit, the truth and heart of God will be revealed concerning all ungodliness. I believe that everyone who worships with us, saved or unsaved, will receive a measure of the Word of God that will enlighten them concerning sin and encourage them to obey the leadership of the Holy Spirit. If you are saved today, you have the Spirit of God *in you* and He will lead you in the way of righteousness. Jesus said in John 16:13, *"However, when He, the Spirit of truth, has come, He will guide you into all truth; for He will not speak on His own authority, but whatever He hears He will speak; and He will tell you things to come."* **Therefore, we cannot compromise because compromise is the first step to disobedience.** This basic truth touches every part of our lives.

It is difficult to resist the temptation and pressures to compromise the standards of God when it involves our marriages, family relationships and close friendships. We often give in to our emotions because of the love that we have for these special people and disregard the commandment of God to obey Him at all times. My dear friend, I want you to know this important truth. **When you compromise your obedience to God, you put yourself into the hands of the devil.** Even with the deep love and affection that I have for my wife Sharlotte, I cannot allow her to interfere with me obeying the Word of the Lord. Similarly, Sharlotte cannot allow me to prevent her from obeying the Word of the Lord. In fact,

60

none of us should ever allow anyone or anything to prevent us from obeying the Word of the Lord! *God demands obedience in every one of His children.*

I Samuel 15. 1-35 outlines the story of Saul and the sin that he committed against the Lord. God told Saul to go over into the camp of the Amalekites and kill everybody and every living thing. The Lord specifically instructed him not to bring anything back: no cattle, no animals, nor anything that was in the land. God wanted Saul to utterly destroy them because He had pronounced His judgement against them. 1 Samuel 15:1-3 gives the specifics concerning the Lord's commandment. The scripture says, *"Samuel also said to Saul, "The LORD sent me to anoint you king over His people, over Israel. Now therefore, heed the voice of the words of the LORD. Thus says the LORD of hosts: 'I will punish Amalek for what he did to Israel, how he ambushed him on the way when he came up from Egypt. Now go and attack Amalek, and utterly destroy all that they have, and do not spare them. But kill both man and woman, infant and nursing child, ox and sheep, camel and donkey.'"* (NKJ) I think we mentioned this before in Chapter 2. These were crystal-clear instructions and could not be misconstrued! However, Saul compromised his integrity with God so that he would receive the glory that rightfully belonged to God.

The Lord is communicating the same message to us. Our Savior is saying, it does not matter how good or glamorous it appears to be, *do not bring back anything from the enemy's camp!* You must leave the devil and his toys alone! My dear friend, if you do not take head, Satan will destroy your life! Saul brought back the finest animals and the spoil of the fallen kingdom, as well as Agag who was the king of the Amalekites. He brought back the very things that God told him not to bring back! As a result of his disobedience and compromise that he made in his heart to forsake the Word of the Lord, the Prophet Samuel pronounced the judgement of God against him. Samuel said to Saul, *"Has the LORD as great delight in burnt offerings and sacrifices, as in obeying the voice of the LORD?"* In other words, do you really think God delights in your burnt offerings and sacrifices? Do you think God wants you to give Him anything more than simple obedience? That is what the Lord is asking each one of us today. What are you *not obeying* as it relates to the commandment of the Lord? We must pay attention to God's words and honor them as the way of life. Proverbs 4:20-22 says, *"My son, give attention to my words; incline your ear to my sayings. Do not let them depart from your eyes; keep them in the midst of your heart; For they are life to those who find them, and health to all their flesh."* (NKJ)

Samuel went on to say, *"Behold, to obey is better than sacrifice, and to heed* [listen and regard] *than the fat of rams..."* **The Lord desires our obedience more than our natural or worldly sacrifices.** In fact, our spiritual obedience is an acceptable sacrifice unto the Lord because *in our obedience* we surrender our will to God's divine will! *Praise the Lord!* Can you hear the voice of the Lord speaking to you through this word? *He is gently asking you: my son or daughter, do you hear me? Are you really listening to me? Are you surrendering your life to me, or are you still trying to call the shots in your life?* Our Savior is saying, *I have already spoken to you and given you commandments. I have shared my heart and given you instructions for your success. I have given you the roadmap to victory and paved the way before you. I have encouraged you and given you an example to follow. I have even given you the Holy Spirit to lead you and empower you to accomplish my will. What is it that is preventing or hindering you from obeying me?* Some people think that they can come and simply give their money in the offering and believe that their financial gift is the primary desire of the Lord in their life. However, the Lord does not want our money because He owns all of the money in the world! Psalms 24.1 declares, *"The earth is the LORD'S, and all its fullness, the world and those who dwell therein."* (NKJ) I praise the Lord because I know that God does not need our money! He wants our life! If worshipping God depended on money, most of the people in the world could not worship Him at all. If our joy depended on finances, many people would never have joy!

I often share this truth with the people that I minister to: *God's presence in my life is the difference that makes the difference in me.* Regardless of where my travels take me, I can always feel His presence! You can drop me in the middle of the jungle in Africa and I will still be able to praise the Lord because *He is there! Hallelujah! God is omnipresence! He is the Lord who is every place at all times!* That is the God that I serve! Who are you serving today? God says, *"Behold, to obey is better than sacrifice, and to heed than the fat of rams…"* If you really want to please God, *just do what He tells you to do!* That reminds me of a story that some of my good friends shared with Sharlotte and me during a Sunday dinner. We were all talking about our children and discussing some of the discipline that we administered to them during their early childhood years. Our friends have two children, a boy and a girl. The girl is about five years older than the boy is. Apparently, their daughter would get into a little mischief at home and at school, and would *always* get caught by her mom! When that happened, our friend said that she would give her a *good spanking!* They shared one particular experience with us that occurred when the girl was around seven years old. Her little brother was only two years old at the time. On that occasion, the little girl got caught doing some more mischief at school. If I remember correctly, she failed to bring her homework home with her from school and told her mother that she did not have any homework to do. Of course she did not know that her mother had already stopped by the school to see if she had homework, *and of course she did have some!* Well, needless to say, she got another *good spanking!* After she got her spanking from her mom, her little brother came up to her crying and said, *"Keasha, just do what they tell you to do and you will not get a spanking! It's not hard!"* Can you believe that a little two-year old boy would have that much sense to share such wholesome advice with his big sister? *I almost fell out of my seat laughing at that story!* Isn't that amazing? Even the smallest children learn the key to success with their parents and the reason for discipline. *Obedience* brings peace and blessings from parents and *disobedience* brings discipline and restrictions. *It is not a mystery at all!* Likewise, if you really want to live in the joy and peace of God, *just do what He tells you to do! It's not hard!* The Apostle John told the church in 1 John 5.3, *"For this is the love of God, that we keep His commandments. And His commandments are not burdensome." (NKJ)* That means they are not hard! *You can obey the Lord and live a life without compromise because YOU have the Holy Spirit residing within you that enables you to do God's will!*

Please allow me to share another thought. If you compromise in the Army you commit *high treason!* Let me explain this point. There is some information that soldiers may possess that can enable the enemy to destroy our total force, if it gets into the enemy's hand. Military forces at war capture enemy soldiers all the time. The captured soldiers are classified as prisoners of war or POWs. When an enemy soldier captures you, they will usually say something enticing to you, to persuade you to compromise your force's battle intelligence and war plans. They will usually promise to treat you well and feed you, or even release you, if you provide them with significant information concerning your commander's war mission. If that *nice* strategy does not work, they sometimes resort to torturing you, pressing you, squeezing you and doing all of sorts of bad things to convince you to give in and give them the information they want. Usually, as soon as you give them the information, they will kill you anyway! Now how does that relate to us? I am glad you asked! We flirt with the devil and often play around in the devil's yard. We play with his toys; we play with his people; we play with his ideas and we reject the ideas of God. We all need to know and understand that everything about the devil is centered on sin, and Romans 6.23 declares that *"the wages of sin is death, but the gift of God is eternal life in Christ Jesus our Lord."*

The scripture is saying, *do not breach or compromise your integrity with God!* You must trust God for everything! You do not have to compromise on your job if you realize that your boss is not really sustaining your life, *God is!* Many Christians are giving all of the power and glory to man because they think that men are keeping them alive. My bible says, *"And you shall remember the LORD your God, FOR IT IS HE WHO GIVES YOU POWER TO GET WEALTH, that He may establish His covenant which He swore to your fathers, as it is this day."* (Deut 8:18 NKJ) Paul said in Acts 17:28, *"For in Him we live, and move, and have our being;.."* You and I did not get up today because we were so careful. We did not get up today because we were so good or righteous. We got up and continue to get up day after day because God gets us up! *"His mercy endures forever!"* Hallelujah to God! The devil is trying to tell you to compromise a little bit. Satan is trying to convince you to be religious, *not righteous.* The devil wants you to come to church on Sunday, but remain uncommitted to anything that glorifies the name of Jesus Christ in the church fellowship. The devil does not mind church membership as long as you never seek to establish a deep relationship with the Lord! My dear friend, the devil does not mind you joining any church so long as you do not become an active member, or become a living witness for Jesus Christ. **Satan wants you to die without making an impact for Jesus Christ in the world!** *His mission is to steal your joy and destroy your life!* Jesus called him a thief and said, *"The thief does not come except to steal, and to kill, and to destroy. I have come that they may have life, and that they may have it more abundantly."* (John 10:10 NKJ) The devil is not trying to play with us, or hurt us, or bruise us up a little here and there. *The devil is trying to kill us!* That is what you need to know today. The Lord is saying, *"Indeed, let God be true but every man a liar."* (Rom 3:4 NKJ) *NO COMPROMISE!*

We seem to compromise everything! Many times we compromise because we do not want to go against the grain. However, if you are going to be a contender for Jesus Christ you must be willing and able to go against the grain! *Glory be to God!* My dear friend, I want you know and consider this thought. God has a whole school of fish that are legitimate contenders for Jesus Christ! Do you know what kind of fish we are? *SALMON!* That is God's fish! Have you ever seen the nature stories and outdoor life programs that come on TV? I love to watch them, although I am no longer a big outdoorsman. My trip to Saudi Arabia during Operation Desert Storm changed my mind on staying outdoors for any substantial period of time. Nevertheless, I remember seeing an episode when they were highlighting the spawning season and journey of the Red Salmon. This story was fascinating to me because it revealed the fact that most species of fish love to swim downstream. They usually desire to go with the flow. They get in the flow and keep going until they reach a desirable or suitable spawning location. It does not take much power to go with the grain or along the same direction as the water current. However, the Salmon is a strong fish that swims upstream to lay her eggs in the most pure water available. The Salmon jumps, swims and struggles to reach its goal upstream, regardless of the difficulty of the currents. It is a determined fish that will not compromise its God-given instinct to spawn upstream during the mating season. *We can take a lesson from the Salmon!* We have been compromising too much and God is challenging each one of us today to stand fast in the Lord and do not compromise with the devil. *"BE NOT CONFORMED TO THIS WORLD, BUT BE YE TRANSFORMED BY THE RENEWING OF YOUR MIND!"* Do not compromise your stand for God!

The prophet Samuel told Saul, *"Behold, to obey is better than sacrifice, and to take heed* [or listen] *than the fats of ram."* The next portion of the scripture outlines the reason for his statement. *"For rebellion is as the sin of witchcraft, and stubbornness is as iniquity and idolatry."* That is what sin is, *Faithless rebellion against the known will of God.* All rebellious acts against God's divine plan for your life are of the highest order of wickedness, ungodliness and evil worship; all of which are against the holiness of God. When you choose not to obey God, it is because you are stubborn. Therefore, Samuel informed Saul *"Because you have rejected the word of the LORD, he also has rejected you from being king."* (1 Sam 15:23 NKJ) What a price to pay for compromising the commandment of God!

Many Christians get upset when the minister preaches the uncut Gospel of Jesus Christ that reveals and uncovers our sinfulness. We get angry and offended when we receive a Word from the Lord through the preacher that is abrasive or cutting to our heart. We often want to attack the messenger rather than receive the message that will deliver us from evil. *Do not kill the messenger!* He or she had nothing to do with the message, except receive it from the Lord and deliver it to you! Usually the people who do those things are *Contestants!* <u>Contenders</u> acknowledge their sin, turn to God in repentance and receive forgiveness of sin to the glory of God. *"Be a Contender, Not Just a Contestant!"* I have strict orders from my sender to tell the Church not to compromise! Why? I'm glad you asked! *Compromise seeks to satisfy and find peace with others rather than God.* Many Christians desire and prefer to have peace amongst each other and be in a war with God! At times, we have things backwards because we have somehow forgotten that God gives life! None of us can give life. God gives us air to breathe. Can any of us give air? God gets us up, heals our sicknesses, delivers us in trouble, sustains us during famine and comforts us in our sorrows. What can anyone else really do for you today that can match what God has done throughout your entire life? *Nothing!* The only thing anyone of us can do for each other is what God enables us to do. David said these words in 2 Samuel 7:22, *"Therefore You are great, O Lord GOD. For there is none like You, nor is there any God besides You, according to all that we have heard with our ears."* (NKJ) Yet, we would rather make amendments and concessions with each other and be out of fellowship with God. Today the Lord is calling for us to change our mind! *NO COMPROMISE!*

My dear friend, I cannot tell you the area(s) in your personal life that you are compromising in. However, I do believe that you know the area(s) because God has already revealed the area(s) to you. You know what the Lord has called you to be, as well as what God has put in you. You also know where God has brought you from and where He desires to take you. You know the Lord has been moving over the altar of your heart. You know the voice of the Lord and you have heard the message that He has been speaking to your heart by the Holy Spirit. In spite of these truths, we often make up our own minds and set the criteria for us to obey His voice and respond to His call in our life. We say, *"Lord when this happens I will respond."* Some have said, *"I will not respond unless you do what I want you to do in my life."* In essence, many of us are trying to make a deal with God that will inspire us to obey His commandments. My dear friend, God is not calling for us to compromise with Him. *The Lord is telling us to obey Him!* Isaiah 1:19 says, *"If you are willing and obedient, you shall eat the good of the land...."* If you are not living a victorious life as a believer and demonstrating Godliness on a daily basis, then you are not qualified to be a witness for Jesus and are living at the level of mediocrity. It is time-out for all of this religion, the phony show and games that we play at the church. It is time to take off the fake masks of hypocrisy and stop the charade that we play out before each other at the church. God wants all of us to be real and sincere in everything that we do for Him. *Let's be real for God!* God wants us to get back to the basics. In the Army, *Basic Training* focuses on accomplishing one primary goal, *DISCIPLINE!* I have already addressed this key point in chapter two. However, you cannot get around it when seeking to raise your spiritual level in the Lord.

Christian contenders are the people who turn away from the world and its sinful desires and remain steadfast in the Lord. Satan has a game for every one of us to play. A lot of men think they have a legitimate game that they employ to get women. However, *nobody has a game that has worked as well as Satan's to ruin your life!* I remember reading a short story entitled *"The Most Dangerous Game"* when I was a kid in elementary school. In that story, a man hunted men as animals because he knew that they were the most cunning and evasive of all mammals on the earth. Likewise, Peter said, *"Be sober, be vigilant; because your adversary the devil walks about like a roaring lion, seeking whom he may devour."* (1 Pet 5:8 NKJ) The end of the devil's game is always death or destruction. *Compromise* is the primary method that Satan uses to convince the believers to give in to his plan. When you give in and compromise with the devil, everything that you touch will go to pits and eventually die. Your marriage will die. Your close relationships will die. Your family will die and anything that is of personal value. Paul told the Roman Church, *"For the wages of sin is death, but the gift of God is eternal life in Christ Jesus our Lord."* (Rom 6:23 NKJ) *Everything that is connected with sin will eventually die.* This is a promise from the Lord, but many Christians do not believe it. Many *Christians* say in their heart, *"Let me see if I can get away with what the devil is putting in my mind. Surely this one time will not kill me or ruin my life, if I am careful."* Consequently, they often find out the hard way that compromising with the devil and sin will take you out and leave you with nothing! Remember Adam and Eve? God gave them strict instructions concerning the rules for living in and maintaining the Garden of Eden. However, they decided in their own mind to disobey His commandment and believe the lie of the devil. Accordingly, their decision cost them eternal life in paradise and caused them to experience spiritual and physical death. *What a price to pay for disobedience!* My dear friend, *your mind* is the spiritual battleground between you and the devil. Therefore, I encourage you to let Christ rule your mind so that you will live in the true victory of Jesus Christ. You must think for yourself. No one can think for you. We all have to make decisions in our life concerning our faithfulness to God. Where you are in the Lord is based upon your own personal decision(s). Remember, *compromising* **with the devil and sin is dangerous and costly.** **[POINT #2]**

The third and final point I need to share with you concerning "NO COMPROMISE" is this: ***compromise in personal and family relations will weaken your faith and hinder your fellowship with God.*** This is a very sensitive point because it addresses the personal relationships that we share with unbelievers. As a prelude to this discussion, let me share this truth. The Lord intends for us to love everybody and share the good news of the Gospel of Jesus Christ with every one that we meet, especially with unbelievers. We are to witness freely and openly to present the hope of eternal life to all that will hear and receive. *God loves everybody and desires for all men to be saved!* That is the given.

However, ***Christians should not knowingly enter into conjugal or courting relationships with unbelievers, regardless of their great personality or desirable traits.*** Joining together with an unbeliever goes against the spiritual standard that God has established for His children. That is why Paul warned the believers in Corinth to avoid getting involved in marital relationships with ungodly people. 2 Corinthians 6:14 says, *"Do not be unequally yoked together with unbelievers."* Your life can be a spiritual wreck if you do! It is very probable that you will fuss and fight with one another primarily because light and darkness cannot coexist peacefully. One is constantly warring against the other. My brother or sister, if you are in a marital relationship with an unbeliever, I encourage you to pray for their salvation. Do not down them or harass them concerning the need to be saved. Just live the Christian life before them and win them by your godly lifestyle. Positive or negative, your life will make the difference in them. In fact, it will either draw them to Christ for salvation or drive them farther away from you. You need to know and accept this truth. Jesus said, *"And you will be hated by all for My name's sake."* (Luke 21:17 NKJ) There is a possibility that your unbelieving spouse will leave you if you become a contender for Jesus Christ. It is our prayer that it does not happen,

70

but it is possible. That may be too great of a price to pay for some Christians. God knows our heart and is greater than all. We trust that He will make the difference in their lives through us. Paul offered his personal advice to new Christians in the Corinthian church that were married to unbelievers. 1 Corinthians 7:12-16 outlines his conversation. *"But to the rest I, not the Lord, say: If any brother has a wife who does not believe, and she is willing to live with him, let him not divorce her. And a woman who has a husband who does not believe, if he is willing to live with her, let her not divorce him. For the unbelieving husband is sanctified by the wife, and the unbelieving wife is sanctified by the husband; otherwise your children would be unclean, but now they are holy. But if the unbeliever departs, let him depart; a brother or a sister is not under bondage in such cases. But God has called us to peace. For how do you know, O wife, whether you will save your husband? Or how do you know, O husband, whether you will save your wife?"* (NKJ) If you are a *contender,* God will make the difference through you!

Another sensitive point surrounds disciplining children when they are disobedient to their parents, or produce undesirable behavior. I love children and have the most wonderful daughter on the face of planet earth! Our daughter, Ebony Nicole Gainous, has literally been a jewel *all of her life.* She is now a young adult (over eighteen years old), and I do not have any bad stories to tell concerning any type of waywardness or rebellion in her. She literally has grown up desiring to please the Lord and her parents. *Ebony is truly a godly child and we praise the Lord for her daily!*

Society has recently set the trend for parents raising and disciplining their children. Corporate punishment has all but been eliminated from the public schools across the nation. Children are seemingly untouchable by parents because they fear the repercussions of a negative report concerning, what is perceived to be, excessive punishment or methods of administering punishment. Christian parents who compromise biblical standards of discipline

71

will put their children's life and future in jeopardy and will concede to whatever the world shapes them to be, good or bad. ***When you raise your children in accordance with the Word of God, the Lord blesses you and your children.*** If they go astray, *and sometimes they do,* the Lord promises that they will have something instilled within them to guide them back to the path of righteousness. Proverbs 22:6 says, *"Train up a child in the way he should go: and when he is old, he will not depart from it."* The bible tells you how to raise godly children. My wife and I are witnesses that *the Lord's way works!* There is no bondage in the Lord's strategy for raising godly kids. *You can follow the rules of the bible and stay out of jail!* Proverbs 14:34 says, *"Righteousness exalteth a nation: but sin is a reproach to any people."* We do not want to raise sinful children because they will become a reproach to us too. If you raise your children by God's standard, you will have peace when the parental storms roll in and you will be able to withstand them by the power of God. You cannot be buddy-buddy with your children and expect to get godly results. ***You must be Mom and Dad at all times!*** Ensure that you love your children and nurture them in the word of God. Instill within them the love and discipline of the Lord. In doing so, you will give them an advantage in life. They will love and thank you for it later. *IT TAKES REAL FAITH TO BE GODLY PARENTS!* Trust the Word of God. Proverbs 3:5-6 says, *"Trust in the LORD with all your heart, and lean not on your own understanding; IN ALL YOUR WAYS ACKNOWLEDGE HIM, and He shall direct your paths."* (NKJ) ***Compromise in personal and family relations will weaken your faith and hinder your fellowship with God.*** **[POINT #3]**

Let me close this chapter with these words of inspiration and encouragement. If you are down today because you have become a victim of the devil's compromising ploy to destroy your life, ***be lifted in the Mighty Name of Jesus!*** Jesus paid the price for all of your sins and offers you a new start and a new beginning in the Lord! He can offer it because He did what none of us could do. Jesus lived in complete obedience to the perfect law of liberty and fulfilled all of the commandments of the Living God! *JESUS CHRIST is our supreme example of a life without compromise!* *JESUS* is our perfect example of a surrendered life to God. He was totally commitment to accomplishing the complete will of God. The Hebrew writer said of the Lord, *"Then said I, Lo, I come (in the volume of the book it is written of me,) to do thy will, O God."* (Heb 10:7) *JESUS* refused to compromise with the devil. He stood His ground through the temptations in the wilderness. He stood His ground through the trials of daily living. He stood His ground through His judgement and condemnation before Herod and Pontius Pilate. *JESUS* stood His ground through the suffering that He endured, *even at the cross of Calvary!* *JESUS CHRIST lived a life that is the paramount example of a total commitment to God!*

When Pilate questioned Jesus during His trial, he thought Jesus would beg for mercy so that He would be released from the vindictive and hateful mob that cried for His crucifixion. However, Jesus remained silent when He stood before Pilate in the judgement hall. Pilate was perplexed by His silence and said to Jesus, *"Are You not speaking to me? Do You not know that I have power to crucify You, and power to release You?"* *Jesus answered, "You could have no power at all against Me unless it had been given you from above."* (John 19:10-11 NKJ) In essence, Jesus was saying, put me on the cross! I am not dying because of any crime or offense that I have committed. I am not dying because of the trumped-up charges these people have indicted me with. *I am dying for the sins of the world!* JESUS was totally committed to God's plan of salvation for lost humanity! He did not back up for any reason, not even to save his own life! *Jesus never compromised His position and purpose for God in the world!*

The mob that watched Him die at Calvary tried to convince Him to come down from the cross to prove that He was the Son of God. I praise God that He stayed on the cross for you and me!

Jesus knew that if He came down from the cross it would be *a fatal compromise* that would ultimately destroy all humanity! If Jesus conceded with the crowd, He never would have shed His precious blood that was the only thing that could remit our sin and satisfy the judgement of God! *I thank God for the Blood of Jesus Christ that has been applied to all of the believers' life!* We are saved today, delivered from sin and healed to the glory of God because Jesus did not compromise! *Hallelujah to the King of Glory!* As a result of His obedience, God raised Jesus up from the grave with all power in Heaven and earth in His hand! God glorified Himself in His resurrection and made the way for all of us to enjoy everlasting life! *We all can become contenders for Jesus Christ and live victoriously to the glory of God! Praise His wonderful Name! JESUS IS THE ULTIMATE EXAMPLE FOR US TO FOLLOW!*

My dear friend, *if you will not compromise with the devil,* you will experience the anointing power of God in your life that will break the yoke of sin in others! The Lord will fill you from top to bottom, inside out! His presence and power will flow through your life and bless others! If you do not compromise, you can overcome evil with good and love those who hate you! *If you will not compromise your position and spiritual integrity with the Lord, God will be for you and with you always!* The Word of God says, *"What shall we then say to these things? If God be for us, who can be against us?"* (Rom 8:31) *"No weapon formed against you shall prosper,....."* (Is. 54.17 NKJ)

Check yourself! Check your life to see if you have been obedient to the commandment of God. The Lord wants you to fulfill your purpose within the body of Jesus Christ. He has given you specific directions to move you from the *contestant* status to the *contender level!* **Can't you hear the Spirit say, "Make a change?"** I encourage you to make a change in your life that will *glorify God* and *crush the devil!* I challenge you to *move from the sideline and get onto the playing field for our Lord!* You can do it because the Lord will strengthen you. Paul said, *"I can do all* *things through Christ who strengthens me."* (Phil 4:13) The Word of God is speaking expressly to the church saying, *"Do not be conformed to this world, but be transformed BY THE RENEWING OF YOUR MIND, that you may prove what is that good and acceptable and perfect will of God."* (Rom 12:2 NKJ) Are you on the Lord's side? Are you willing to obey the voice of the Lord in your life? God is calling today for your personal obedience. If you have been compromising with the devil, <u>STOP IT RIGHT NOW</u>! *Today*, God says to repent! That means for you to turn around and go in another direction. I can hear the wonderful words of the Apostle John encouraging the members of the church, saying, *"This is the message which we have heard from Him and declare to you, that God is light and in Him is no darkness at all. If we say that we have fellowship with Him, and walk in darkness, we lie and do not practice the truth. But if we walk in the light as He is in the light, we have fellowship with one another, and <u>the blood of Jesus Christ His Son cleanses us from all sin</u>. If we say that we have no sin, we deceive ourselves, and the truth is not in us. If we confess our sins, He is faithful and just to forgive us our sins and to cleanse us from all unrighteousness."* (I Jn 1:5-9 NKJ) <u>*MAKE THE CHANGE TODAY! RENEW YOUR MIND!*</u>

Let me say this to you while you are before the Lord. The devil will try to convince you that you have time, or this is not the right time to make a commitment to God. He is coming against you even now to take away the seed of faith the Lord has planted in you by reading this book. Please do not allow the devil to win this battle in your life. God has already spoken to your heart and has told you what you need to do in order to live in the victory of Jesus Christ. The Lord has even showed you how to get to where you need to be in Him! *Make a decision to make a stand for Jesus Christ!* DO NOT COMPROMISE THE STANDARD OF GOD! Everything that I have shared in this book is written to get you to think about your life and motivate you to love the Lord more. *"Do not be conformed to this world, but be transformed by the renewing of your mind."* The message is designed to get you to respond to the Spirit of Jesus Christ. It is about receiving deliverance and the blessings of God! Do not accept a mediocre lifestyle as a believer. Do not compromise your witness for Jesus Christ: in your marriage; in your relationship with your loved ones; when raising your children; on your job; in your home; or any area of your life. ***God wants to bless every facet and fiber of your life!*** Moses told the nation of Israel, *"For if you carefully keep all these commandments which I command you to do: to love the LORD your God, to walk in all His ways, and to hold fast to Him; then the LORD will drive out all these nations from before you, and you will dispossess greater and mightier nations than yourselves."* [You will conquer them] God said, *"If you will obey my voice and follow me, Every place on which the sole of your foot treads shall be yours: from the wilderness and Lebanon, from the river, the River Euphrates, even to the Western Sea, shall be your territory. No man shall be able to stand against you; the LORD your God will put the dread of you and the fear of you upon all the land where you tread, just as He has said to you."* (Deut 11:22-25 NKJ) The Lord said, *"Behold, I set before you this day a blessing and a curse; A BLESSING, IF YE OBEY the commandments of the LORD your God, which I command you this day: And A CURSE, IF YE WILL NOT OBEY the commandments of the LORD your God, but turn aside out of the way which I command you this day, to go after other gods, which you have not known."* (Deut. 11:26-28) God pleaded with Israel to turn from sin and obey the commandment of the Lord. Isaiah 1:18-20 records this dialogue that God made to Israel, *"Come now, and let us reason together,"* says the LORD, *"Though your sins are like scarlet, they shall be as white as snow; though they are red like crimson, they shall be as wool. IF YOU ARE WILLING AND OBEDIENT, you shall eat the good of the land; But if you refuse and rebel, you shall be devoured by the sword; for the mouth of the LORD has spoken."* GOD SAID IT! In other words, IF YOU DO NOT COMPROMISE you will enjoy the finer things that the Lord has prepared for His obedient children. If you refuse to obey, you will suffer the judgement and punishment of God. My dear friend, don't you want to enjoy the blessings of God and eat the good of the land? Don't you want God to flow through your life? Then DO NOT COMPROMISE! That is what our Savior is telling us. Regardless of the number and magnitude of your personal issues, or the difficulty of your circumstances, *do not compromise your spiritual integrity with God!* Jesus did not compromise. Hebrews 12:2-4 encourages us to *"look unto Jesus, the author and finisher of our faith, WHO FOR THE JOY THAT WAS SET BEFORE HIM ENDURED THE CROSS, DESPISING THE SHAME, and has sat down at the right hand of the throne of God. For consider Him who endured such hostility from sinners against Himself, lest you become weary and discouraged in your souls. You have not yet resisted to bloodshed, striving against sin."* (NKJ)

Deuteronomy chapter 28 outlines all of the blessings that every believer can expect to receive when they *faithfully obey* the word of the Lord. Did you notice that I used the term *"faithfully obey?"* Faithful obedience is what is required in the life of every Christian contender for Jesus Christ. You cannot reach the level of a contender without *faithful obedience!* If you are faithful, the Lord promises in the Word, *"Eye has not seen, nor ear heard, nor have entered into the heart of man the things which God has prepared for those who love Him."* (1 Cor 2:9 NKJ)

My dear friend, I really want you to think about your relationship with the Lord and answer three questions in your heart. First of all, *Where are you in the Lord?* Is God pleased with your life and your commitment that you have shown, *not spoken,* but shown towards Him in your daily lifestyle? Secondly, *Is there anyone or anything competing with the Lord in your life?* Is there anyone or anything between you and your Savior? Finally, *If the people who know you and work around you were asked to give a report on you, will there be anything mentioned in their statement that will bear witness to the fact that you are a believer?* I certainly hope the evidence is strong enough for them to say that you are truly a Child of the King and a Contender for

77

Jesus Christ! Only you know the true answers to these questions. *"Be a Contender, Not Just a Contestant!"* - <u>**NO COMPROMISE**</u>!

Chapter IV

FIGHT TO WIN!

"Therefore I run thus: not with uncertainty. Thus I fight: not as one who beats the air. But I discipline my body and bring it into subjection, lest, when I have preached to others, I myself should become disqualified." **(1 Cor 9:26-27 NKJ)**

Now that you have made up your mind to be steadfast in the Lord and *will not compromise* with the devil on any point, **_LET'S GET READY TO RUMBLE!_** *It is time to fight the devil and engage in spiritual warfare!* I want you to repeat these words in your spirit to prepare you for this chapter: *"FIGHT TO WIN!"* That is the message for you this day and that is what every believer in Jesus Christ must be willing to do. *You have to fight to win!* God gave me this thought to share with you in this book. When you think of the struggles and all of the obstacles that we encounter just living, you must come to grips that you must be a fighter to survive! We encounter the devil on every side. It seems as though everywhere you turn, regardless of the day, Satan is there to aggravate you and stop you from accomplishing the will of God in your life. The devil is trying to destroy you and put heavy burdens on you to discourage you. He is trying to cast you down and press you down so that you cannot get up. However, God told me to tell you and Christians everywhere to *"Fight to Win!"* It is a simple statement of encouragement but it is packed with *spiritual power!* Praise the Mighty Name of Jesus!

Webster's Dictionary provides the following definitions for the word *fight*: *"to contend in battle or physical combat; a hostile encounter; to strive to overcome a person by blows or weapons; to engage in boxing;"* *Fight* also means *"to put forth a determined effort to conquer an enemy; to attempt to prevent the success or effectiveness of."* A *fight* is *"a struggle to endure and overcome an obstacle or a legitimate opponent."* *Fight* is also defined as *"the strength or disposition to struggle for a goal or an objective."* That is what I mean by *fight!* **In order to fight, you must be a fighter! Before you can qualify as a fighter, you must first have some FIGHT in you!** Praise the Lord! You will never fight if there is no fight in you! Consequently, you will never win a spiritual fight or battle against the devil if you tuck tail and run every time he challenges you in your life. Every now and then you have to execute a pivot move, turn around and deliver a *spiritual blow* to repel his attacks. My dear friend, I want you to know that God has called all of His children to be fighters! *Are you a fighter today? Are you willing to stand up against Satan? GOD IS CALLING YOU TO BE A FIGHTER!*

When you consider the definition of the word *fighter,* you can determine if you qualify as one or not. *A fighter is a warrior or a soldier.* I have already mentioned to you that I am a soldier in the United States Army Reserves (USAR). I put on my Battle Dress Uniform (BDU) every month to proudly serve my country. I am a special officer because I have a dual commission. I am a commissioned officer in the USAR and *a commissioned soldier in the Army of the Lord!* I am a fighter and I am on the battlefield for my Lord and Savior Jesus Christ! *Bless His wonderful name!* One of the most popular church songs that I remember singing at Lawson Temple Church of God In Christ, while I attended Oklahoma State University, was *"I'm a Soldier In the Army of the Lord!"* That was a powerful song! Some of the verses included statements like: *"I am a sanctified warrior in the Army of the Lord." "I have my war clothes on in the Army of the Lord." "I am a Holy Ghost soldier In the Army of the Lord...."* The song challenged me to be a faithful soldier for Jesus Christ.

When you look at history, you discover that every great nation was born out of struggle and a great fight. I will never forget the statement that General George S. Patton made of himself. He said, *"I am a soldier. I fight where I am told and I win where I fight."* I can feel the power and influence of those words today. No wonder he was such a great and beloved leader.

Do you have that testimony today? Do those words speak the sentiments of your heart? *"...I fight where I am told...."* That means that I am not picking my ground every time. Sometimes I have to fight in places that I do not choose or desire to fight in. I am sometimes forced to fight when it is not convenient to fight. However, the Lord is telling us that wherever you are, wherever the devil shows up, you must be able to fight and win! Satan may show up in your home, in your marriage, on your job or any place he can produce a negative result or destructive effect. Wherever the devil shows up, you must be prepared to fight in that spot!

Many believers have fallen for the false idea that the Christian life is easy and simple. Contrary to this belief, the Christian life is not to be lived on a playground, but on a battleground. In fact, the Christian life must be lived on the battlefield for our Lord. *Are you a Christian soldier?* Our foes consist of the devil and his angels. The Apostle Paul reminded the believers of Ephesus that we are constantly engaged in battle against a legitimate foe and enemy. The devil is real and he definitely is not a toy for Christians to play with! If you have ever encountered real combat with the devil, you know that he is real. The devil is as real today as God is. The devil is as viable today in people's lives as God ever will be. That is why the Apostle Peter told the church to *"Be sober, be vigilant; because your adversary the devil walks about like a roaring lion, seeking whom he may devour."* (1 Pet 5:8 NKJ) Peter told the believers to *"resist him, steadfast in the faith...."* (1 Pet 5:9a NKJ) Steadfastness in anything means a determined effort. If you remain steadfast in your faith toward God and fight against the temptations and schemes of the devil you will be a *contender for Jesus Christ!*

In case you did not know, there is a tremendous war that is going on in the world. We are engaged in a spiritual battle for the souls of men. The devastating effects of sin are everywhere. Every direction you turn, you see the evidence of warfare between the living and the dead, between right and wrong, between the warriors of God and the battlers of Satan. The devil is a legitimate foe in our lives! If you do not believe this to be a true statement, just look around at this world and observe the devastating effects that Satan and sin have produced in the lives of men. For instance, you have little five and six year-old kids carrying guns to school and killing other innocent children. Teenagers, who openly threaten their teachers and peers at school, promise to get revenge over them and anyone who will stand up for them. Every year the news informs us of horrible acts of hatred that are committed at public and private schools across our nation. These acts range from random incidents of specific violence against an individual student or teacher, to mass murders that take the lives of many.

Look on the streets in every major city and see the deplorable effects illegal drugs, alcoholism, sexual immorality and hate crimes produce in our communities. Pull up some of the statistics on the family and hold your breath when you discover that adults are committing incest and other unthinkable acts of sin with their own children! The devil is real and he does not care about you or me! Look around. Look on the acknowledged bad streets in your city and see how people's lives have been battered and broken by the devil and sin. People are strung out on dope and will do *anything* to get money to support their addiction. *The streets of our cities across the nation are filled with the living dead!* However, the effects of sin are not limited to the socially and economically deprived sections of our cities! You can go to the ritzy neighborhoods, the *"Pill Hills" – "Beverly Hills"* and all of the rest of the aristocratic areas and find rich folks who are strung out on crack cocaine and other high-end drugs. You will discover that some of the most atrocious sins, of all types and nature, are committed in the *upscale neighborhoods* and suburbs of our cities. *No one is exempt from the disastrous effects of sin, or the vicious attacks of the devil!*

The evidence of Satan's strategy to destroy mankind is everywhere. Look at some of the other statistics that are in the world today. Forty years ago most couples that were married stayed married to their chosen spouse until death. Divorce was almost unheard of and was the rare exception in our society.

Today, an astounding number of marital relationships are failing before the fifth year of marriage. It used to be that you could get married and hang in there during the tough times. However, today, couples are dissolving their marriages because of minor disagreements and selfish reasons, not to mention rampant adultery and unfaithfulness. Satan has also taken our children and has turned them against their own parents! Children have become disobedient and disrespectful to parental authority. They have become rebellious against their own parents, the very people who are taking care of them every day!

The devil has used worldly standards to paint a picture that defines success as being something attainable only through economic wealth and achieving an elite social status. Consequently, people are running wild and killing themselves chasing after worldly riches. Millions of people are dissatisfied with themselves, and life in general, because they feel that they do not measure up to the social standards of success in the world. However, my dear friend, you and I do not have to possess all of the worldly things unregenerate men are chasing after to fit in or feel special. Our value is not given to us by the world. *Our value comes from the Lord! God makes your life and my life valuable!* How do you feel about yourself? Who do you turn to for encouragement and value? The devil is running so rampant, and getting into the minds of God's people so strongly, that many Christians are unable to war a good battle against him. The Lord challenges us to fight the devil to the bitter end! Do not allow him to take control over you. Give God the reins of your life and when you face the devil in a conflict you will be successful. *Praise His Holy Name!*

Please consider this thought: *"**Life is one big fight!**"* Isn't that the truth? *Life is one big fight!* Sometimes we have to fight to get up in the morning to go to work so that we can earn money to pay our bills. We stay up all night watching TV, knowing that we need to go to bed so that we will be rested for the next day. The devil causes many Christians to skip morning worship on Sunday morning by convincing them to stay up, or out, all night Saturday. The devil does not care how he gets you; he just wants to get you! Sometimes I stay up so late watching ESPN's *Sports Center* on work nights that the alarm clock almost falls off the side of the bed trying to get me up for work the next morning. Sometimes you have to fight to go to work, or fight to keep quiet on your job because you know that you cannot say everything that is on your mind to your boss! Sometimes you have to fight so that you will not say something to someone that you know has intentionally been rude to you. *Life is one big fight!* Many times, you have to fight and dig to pay your bills. *Life is one big fight!* Sometimes you have to fight to stay in your marriage. You do not have to *physically fight* one another. However, you will at times have to fight to do what the Lord is telling you to do in your relationship to enrich your marriage. Sometimes godly parents have to fight to prevent themselves from over disciplining their children when they have committed some incredibly crazy or stunning act. *Life is one big fight!* The Lord wants you to know that it is all right to get into a tussle or a fight in your life because *Life is one big fight!* However, if you are going to fight, you want to be successful.

I will never forget my childhood days growing up in Lawton, OK. I remember having to fight from time to time to defend my honor or family name. Every neighborhood had a bully that always picked on the kids he knew he could intimidate and beat up. The only people the bully did not pick on were the ones he was unsure that he could beat up, or the ones who had a big brother or sister that would beat him up if he bothered their little brother or sister! I want you to know that the devil is the spiritual bully in the world today. He is trying to intimidate all believers and discourage them from fulfilling their purpose for Jesus Christ in the world. The Apostle Peter said *"your adversary the devil walks about like a roaring lion, seeking whom he may devour..."* He is the neighborhood bully and the whole world is his neighborhood! However, God will give you something that will enable you to triumph over the bully. He has given us a *great Big*

Brother who has already defeated the devil in the world! *Thank God for Jesus!*

The Lord gave me three things to share with you that will help you in your battle with the devil. If you receive this advice, you will be or become a *legitimate contender for Jesus Christ.* First of all, *do not fight for the sake of fighting!* **Fight to Win!** Why are you going to get into a fight if you are not going to win? That would be crazy, borderline insane! Why would anyone want to engage in battle with someone when they know that they are going to get whooped and beat down? Why should I pick a fight that I know that I cannot win? *If you are going to fight, fight to win!* A lot of people just fight to get people off of their back. Some people show up and fight so that nobody will call them a chicken. Some people jump into fights for no apparent or logical reason: just fighting to be fighting. If we look at the example of Jesus and the many threatening encounters that he had with the religious leaders of His day, we find that He never had to look for trouble, it always found Him! Jesus did not have to go around picking a fight or looking for a fight. Every time He turned around somebody challenged Him concerning His authority, His message and demonstrated power that He used to heal the sick and raise the dead. Jesus knew that *Life is one big fight!* Our Lord encouraged His disciples to remain faithful in the fight when He said, *"These things I have spoken to you, that in Me you may have peace. In the world you will have tribulation; but be of good cheer, I have overcome the world."* (John 16:33 NKJ) *Do not fight just to be fighting! Fight to win!*

Let us consider what Paul said in our theme scripture for this chapter. 1 Corinthians 9:26-27 says, *"I therefore so run, not as uncertainly..."* Paul was clear and sure about his race and purpose for Jesus Christ in the world. Paul declares that he was not operating or working in the dark. He went on to say; *"so fight I, not as one that beateth the air..."* Paul was saying that he was not just swinging aimlessly and randomly in the air. He was not swinging just to be swinging like so many of us do, or have done.

He had a target that he was striving to hit! I remember a few times when I stood helplessly by and witnessed the neighborhood bully beating up some poor kid and seeing the kid just swing aimlessly in any direction when the bully stopped hitting him. It seemed that the kid just swung out hoping that he would accidentally hit his target and stop the beating. Unfortunately, nobody was there but the air! Paul is telling us to calibrate and put our sights on the target before we expend a round or blow! Some of us are just swinging. We are not engaging the target because we do not know who the target is! Today, the Lord is saying do not swing as one that is beating the air. If you are going to deliver a blow, then deliver the blow to a legitimate target. In boxing they use the term *loading up* to describe a very successful blow that fighters deliver during a boxing match. We also used the same term in our neighborhood. I remember when we would all stand around and watch a good fight. We kind of made ourselves judges and would declare the winner of the fight when it was over. *In Lawton, Oklahoma, whoever delivered the best blow, or series of blows, won the fight!* More importantly, *whoever got hit in the eye automatically lost the fight!* Nobody could ever fully recover from a blow to the eye. You could get hit on the chin or in the jaw and recover. However, when you got hit in the eye everything stopped and everybody started hollering and laughing at you because you were immediately declared the loser! They laughed because your opponent *loaded up on you!* The Lord is trying to tell you and me today to *load up on the devil!* However, right now the devil is loading up on us and we are allowing him to win the fight in critical areas of our life. *Stop allowing the devil to load up on you! Today God is saying that YOU CAN WIN THE FIGHT! YOU NEED TO "FIGHT TO WIN!"*

In essence, Paul is saying, do not just go through the motions when you battle the devil. You need to fight knowing that God has given you purpose and direction so that you will be successful in your combat with Satan. In 1 Timothy 6.12, Paul exhorts Timothy to *"Fight the good fight of faith, lay hold on eternal life, to which you were also called and have confessed the good confession in the presence of many witnesses."* Please allow me to paraphrase the first portion of that scripture. Paul basically said, Timothy, do not just be out there. Do not just show up. Fight in the good fight of faith so that you will one day receive the blessings of eternal life. Do not involve or entangle yourself with things that do not really matter. In other words, *do not sweat the dumb stuff!* Do not fight just to be fighting. *Fight where it counts!* **My dear friend, the only place that counts is in God!** Always remember: *DO NOT FIGHT FOR THE SAKE OF FIGHTING!* *FIGHT TO WIN!*

The second point I want to share with you is this; *you must be strong in the Lord and powerful to win the fight!* Ephesians 6:10-11says, *"Finally, my brethren, be strong in the Lord..."* You notice where Paul commanded the church to focus its strength? *In the Lord!* Do not seek to be strong in your own strength. *Be strong in the Lord!* That is why so many of us are losing our battles. We often try to use our own strength to fight against an enemy that is stronger than we are. My dear friend, if we do not have God with us we cannot defeat the devil! *You cannot beat the devil by yourself!* You cannot defeat the devil in your own strength because your strength runs out! Jesus told Paul, *"My grace is sufficient for you, for My strength is made perfect in weakness."* Paul responded by saying, *"Therefore most gladly I will rather boast in my infirmities, that the power of Christ may rest upon me. Therefore I take pleasure in infirmities, in reproaches, in needs, in persecutions, in distresses, for Christ's sake. For when I am weak, then I am strong."* (2 Cor 12:9-10 NKJ) If you are going to be a contender for Jesus Christ today, you need to be strong in the Lord and you need to be powerful.

Paul said, *"Finally, my brethren, be strong in the Lord and in the power of His might. Put on the whole armor of God..."* In other words, do not just put anything on, and do not put on part of the armor and leave yourself exposed. *"Put on the WHOLE ARMOR OF GOD that you may be able to stand against the wiles of the devil."* Paul went on to say; *"For we do not wrestle against flesh and blood..."* That is a critical point! We are not fighting against men. You and I are not fighting against any particular man or woman in the world. *We are fighting against the devil!"* The church will be effective in its battle against Satan when the *church members* stop biting and devouring one another. If you are having marital conflicts, and all couples experience them from time to time, you must know that your husband or wife is not the origin of your problem. Satan is! The devil is influencing and prompting your spouse to do things that will break the peace and oneness in your relationship! In the other areas of your life, you need to know and understand that it is not your child, co-worker or any one else that you are feuding with. It is the devil that is motivating them to do things against you to disturb your peace. Therefore, we are not fighting against one another, *"but against principalities, against powers, against the rulers of the darkness of this age, against spiritual hosts of wickedness in the heavenly places."* That is what our battle is against!

Carnal minded people always try to fight a spiritual war with natural and carnal weapons. You may be saying, *What do you mean preacher?* Let me share this thought. There are many Christians in the world trying to fight an invisible enemy with carnal measures and methods. They do not realize that they are not in a carnal battle, but a spiritual battle! Likewise, if you fight the devil with carnal methods you will never win the battle; you will always be a failure, because you are not fighting according to the rules of God. The devil can put a stronghold on your life that cannot be broken by your strength. Paul reminded the Corinthian church that *"the weapons of our warfare are not carnal..."* Meaning they are not from the world. *"But mighty through God..."* They are enabled by God, *"to the pulling down of strong holds;"* (2 Cor. 10.4) Has the devil put up a stronghold in your life? If you fight with the Spirit of God you will pull down the strongholds of the devil! If you fight in accordance with the Word of God you will be successful. When the wives stop fighting against their husbands and start praying for them, with spiritual warfare, they will be successful. Likewise, when the husbands stop battering their wives and start loving them in the same manner that Jesus Christ loves the church, they will be successful. When Christian parents start disciplining their kids according to Biblical principles, they will discover that their children will be obedient. The Bible says that *"Foolishness is bound in the heart of a child; but the rod of correction shall drive it far from him."* (Prov 22:15) My dear friend, I am successful in my battle against the devil because I am fighting the way the Lord told me to fight! I have joy in my life because I am fighting the way God told me to fight! I have peace in the midst of total chaos because I am fighting the way God told me to fight! I want you to know that you will be successful when you make up your mind to do things the way the Lord says to do them! You will also have joy and peace if you fight the way the Lord tells you to fight! Paul said, ***"the weapons of our warfare are not carnal, but mighty through God..."*** I am successful in my quest to remain a legitimate contender for Jesus Christ because I am fighting the way God told me to fight *and I'm using His weapons! I AM FIGHTING TO WIN! Hallelujah!* It is not because I am so good. *It is because God is so great!* God enables my weapons, ***"to the pulling down of strong holds!"***

The spiritual weapons of God will do more than pull down the strong holds that Satan puts up in your life. Paul said, they will ***"cast down imaginations!"*** You may be asking yourself, *"What does Paul mean by that?"* I am glad you asked! The Greek word for *imaginations* in this scripture is *logismos* (log-is-mos'). *Logismos* is defined as a computation or logical reasoning within the natural conscience that is devoid of truth. Therefore, it is based upon a lie, which must involve the devil. Jesus said, *"The devil...was a murderer from the beginning, and does not stand in the truth, because there is no truth in him. When he speaks a lie, he speaks from his own resources, for he is a liar and the father of it."* (John 8:44 NKJ) The devil wants to control your imagination so that he will control your mind. If he has the control of your mind then he has control of you! Proverbs 23:7 says, *"For as he thinks in his heart, so is he."* (NKJ)

Imagining is anticipating nothing! However, sinful imaginations can and will destroy your life! In fact, ungodly imaginations create sin and sin brings forth and produces death in the lives of God's people. Today, Christians are imagining things that have caused them to live defeated and spiritually dysfunctional lives. Christians are allowing the devil to fill their minds with wrenching and perverted thoughts that are causing them to suffer mental anguish and unbearable stress. Today, many Christians are experiencing failed health and sicknesses that are directly related to stress caused by sinful imaginations. My dear friend, you must know and realize that *everything that is connected to sin dies!* Christian marriages are failing, Christian homes are breaking up and the lives of many born-again believers in Jesus Christ are being destroyed because of sin and ungodly imaginations. A number of Christians imagine their spouses are unfaithful because many of them are unsaved. Some Christians imagine their spouse does not love them because they do not do everything that they desire, when they want them to do it. Many of us imagine that something bad is bound to happen if we experience more than two weeks of everything going right. People who are in poor physical condition imagine that every little nagging or unexplainable pain that they feel is the beginning stage of an incurable disease or serious medical problem. *Imagining is anticipating nothing!*

Christians set things up in their minds and harbor negative thoughts that eat away at their inner man and eventually hold them captive. The devil will influence you to think negative and destructive thoughts that you should not consider, or entertain as a believer, concerning people and life in general. The devil will speak to your mind and convince you to give up and quit because he says that your situation is hopeless. Satan will try to tell you that there is no way that you can overcome the challenging obstacle(s) in your life. He will tell you that a particular problem or obstacle is too great for you and will make you say in your own heart that you cannot conquer it. The truth of the matter is that we all face obstacles that challenge our faith and peace with God! However, you can overcome any obstacle by the power of God!

The Apostle Paul said, *"I can do all things through Christ who strengthens me."* (Phil 4:13 NKJ) *Hallelujah to God!* The weapons of our warfare will cast down *every imagination* and worldly thought the devil will suggest to you that is against the holiness of God. *He can bring you the bone but you do not have to take it! Stop imagining and start living to the Glory of God! Hallelujah!* Today the Lord says, *"FIGHT TO WIN!"* Paul went on to say, *"Casting down imaginations and every high thing that exalteth itself against the knowledge of God, and bringing into captivity every thought to the obedience of Christ..."* My dear friend, protect your mind from sinful imaginations. Remember: **YOU MUST BE STRONG IN THE LORD AND POWERFUL TO WIN THE FIGHT!**

The third and final point that I will share concerning your quest to fight a good fight for Jesus Christ is this: *you must be highly disciplined to win the fight!* There is that word again: <u>*discipline*</u>. *You just cannot get away from it if you really intend to be a contender for Jesus Christ!* **Discipline is a baseline requirement for every true contender! DISCIPLINE SEPARATES THE CONTENDERS FROM THE CONTESTANTS!** The Bible commands us in Psalms 46.10 to *"Be still and know that I am God."* It takes discipline to be still and wait on the Lord. We often attempt to implement our own timelines and get in front of the Lord. We get impatient and try to tell God how and when He has to deliver us. Jesus said, *"In your patience possess ye your souls."* (Lu. 21.19) You must be very disciplined to be victorious in Jesus Christ. Paul said, ***"I keep under my body."* (KJV) *"I discipline my body and bring it into subjection...."* (NKJ)** Paul said that he subdued and conquered every ungodly desire and motive that the devil brought to him. He declared that he conquered them ***"lest, when I have preached to others, I myself should become disqualified."* (1 Cor 9:27 NKJ)** Today, the Lord is telling us that we cannot be hypocrites. You must be disciplined to live a victorious life for Jesus Christ before the world. People are going to believe what they see you do more than what they hear you say. *What you say must match up with what you do! Praise the Lord!*

A good soldier must possess discipline to fulfill his or her mission and purpose in the United States Army. I have already mentioned that I served as the company commander of Headquarters and Headquarters Company of the 51st Signal Battalion during Operations Desert Shield and Desert Storm. There was nothing glamorous about fighting in the Persian Gulf. Every day I thanked God for keeping my soldiers and me safe from all of the impending dangers that threatened us throughout our deployment. One of my Signal platoons (MOBTAC) provided direct communications support for LTG Frederick Franks at the VII Corps (US) tactical command post (Corps TAC CP). My lieutenant always briefed me on the current tactical situation and future operational events when I visited the VII Corps TAC CP. I had friends that worked in the G2 Intelligence cell and the G3 Operations cell. Therefore, I was always aware of our war strategy to defeat the Iraqi Army. My friends showed me the operations plan and the actual battle plans that outlined the axis and routes of advancement for our allied forces. The battle plans revealed the various enemy objectives that our forces targeted for destruction. It was an integrated battle plan that consisted of closely coordinated air strikes by the Air Force; Tomahawk Cruise Missiles attacks that were launched by our Naval Forces; Air Assault missions and a massive ground attack. The intent and purpose of every action that our coalition force executed was designed to defeat and destroy the Iraqi forces on the battlefield! I saw the forecast timelines, the coordinated fire lines and the fire missions that our Field Artillery units executed to provide cover and concealment for our ground forces. It was a magnificent battle plan that the coalition forces executed to the minute detail! However, if any unit failed to follow their specific orders, they could compromise or jeopardize the entire plan and cause thousands of soldiers to die during the battle. *You must have discipline to be successful in the battle!* There were times when the subordinate field commanders knew that the greatest weight of the enemy forces were in their sector. There is always the fear of being overrun or defeated by your enemy. In spite of overwhelming odds, some commanders receive orders to hold their position *at all cost, regardless of the extreme challenge the unit may be facing! Sometimes you must stay there, even if you have to die in place, because the success of the overall battle may be hinging on your unit providing a pivoting point for the entire force!*

Can you imagine receiving an order like that? I am here to tell you that men are sending soldiers out to battle enemy forces like that every day! More incredible than that is the fact that *GOOD SOLDIERS will fulfill the orders of their commanders, even at the risk of losing their own life!* Are you a good soldier for Jesus Christ? Are you obeying the orders of your *spiritual commander?* Are you disciplined enough to go where the Lord tells you to go and do what the Lord tells you to do, *even if it endangers your life, or causes you to suffer loss?* Paul challenged Timothy to *"endure hardness as a good soldier of Jesus Christ! No one engaged in warfare entangles himself with the affairs of this life, that he may please him who enlisted him as a soldier."* (2 Tim 2. 3-4 NKJ) Paul penned these powerful words to Timothy when he was in prison watching as Nero's chopping block was being oiled and greased for his own execution. Paul knew that he was about to die because of his bold witness for Jesus Christ! Nevertheless, he took his waning hours to write his second epistle to Timothy to command his beloved son in the ministry to *"be strong in the grace that is in Christ Jesus!"* In essence, Paul reminded Timothy of the fact that every believer in Christ is called to be a warrior on the battlefield! Paul is telling you and me that no one can be a good soldier for Jesus Christ if they are entangled in the affairs of this life. You cannot allow yourself to become trapped and twisted by the things of the world, *that you may please him who enlisted you as a soldier of Jesus Christ.* My dear friend, you are not living to please the world! *God created you to worship, to praise and glorify His Name!* You must love Him

93

more than anyone or anything else in this world! I often share with my church congregation that *I am a recruiter for my Savior and CCP is a recruiting station for believers in Jesus Christ! We live and we die for Him! Jesus is the Captain of our salvation and spiritual commander on the battlefield!* Praise the Lord! Remember: **YOU MUST BE HIGHLY DISCIPLINED TO WIN THE FIGHT!**

Let me close this chapter with these words of encouragement and inspiration. ***WE ARE CHRISTIAN SOLDIERS! WE FIGHT WHERE THE LORD PLACES US AND WE WIN WHERE WE FIGHT, BECAUSE GOD IS FOR US!*** Romans 8.31 says, *"What then shall we say to these things? If God is for us, who can be against us?"* (NKJ) ***JESUS IS OUR EXAMPLE!*** He came down to earth as the warrior of God, *the Lion from the tribe of Judah!* Jesus Christ was the best prizefighter and warrior that God ever placed on the battlefield! ***HE FOUGHT WHERE GOD TOLD HIM TO FIGHT and HE WON WHERE HE FOUGHT!*** *Hallelujah To The King Of Glory!* God picked a hill that *they called Calvary* to execute His divine judgement and righteous indignation against sin. Jesus was crucified on an old rugged cross to provide an eternal and perpetual atonement for our sins! The cross was an instrument of pain and suffering! The crucifixion was an event of agony and death! *At the cross of Calvary,* Jesus fought the battle that we could not win and paid the debt that we could not pay! *At Calvary,* God shed His mercy and grace upon the world! *At Calvary,* the love and glory of God was revealed and our victory won! *JESUS IS THE REASON FOR MY JOY!* He did for you and me what we could not do for ourselves! *HE DELIVERED US FROM OUR SINFUL NATURE!* That is why my life is blessed! That is why my marriage and home are blessed! *JESUS DIED FOR OUR SINS!* He fought and died so that we could have life, peace and receive joy in the Holy Ghost! *Bless His Holy Name!*

My dear friend, *Jesus is telling you "FIGHT TO WIN!"* **Are you a fighter?** You must never give up because He did not give up! It would be understandable for you or anyone that is a believer to give up and quit, if Jesus did not win the battle over sin. Consequently, *Jesus suffered and died for our sins! He was hung-up for our hang-ups! We can rejoice because WE HAVE A SAVIOR! Hallelujah!* The Lord said, *"When you pass through the waters, I will be with you; and through the rivers, they shall not overflow you. When you walk through the fire, you shall not be burned, nor shall the flame scorch you. For I am the LORD your God, the Holy One of Israel, YOUR SAVIOR..."* (Isa 43:2-3 NKJ) *Praise the Lord!*

Are you thankful for what Jesus did for you? *Have you really thought about what He did for you?* When you were on your way to hell, before you loved Him. The bible says *"when we were still without strength, in due time Christ died for the ungodly,'* and *'God demonstrated His own love toward us, in that while we were still sinners, [stinking in our sins] Christ died for us."* (Rom 5. 6,8 NKJ) Nobody but Jesus was able to deliver us from our sins! We could not do it! Moses could not do it! Abraham could not do it! The Old Testament Prophets could not do it! David could not do it! *NOBODY BUT JESUS could save us and deliver us from our sin!* I love Him today because He did what I could not do. *He delivered me from the consequence and penalty of my sin!*

My dear friend, you may have been thinking about giving up today before you read this particular chapter. You may be getting tired of fighting! The heat of the battle may have brought you to the point of total exhaustion. You may be at the end of your rope and ready to let go! You may even feel as though your situation is dead and you are about to expire. The devil is trying to convince you that it is futile and senseless for you to keep on struggling. *I want you to rebuke that thought and know that God specializes in making dead situations come alive!* The bible says, *"We are troubled on every side, yet not distressed; we are perplexed, but not in despair; Persecuted, but not forsaken; cast down, but not destroyed..."* (2 Cor 4:8-9) *HALLELUJAH! THANK YOU LORD! YOU CAN MAKE IT THROUGH YOUR*

95

STORM! YOU WILL MAKE IT BY THE POWER OF THE LIVING GOD! WE ARE VICTORIOUS PEOPLE! The devil is trying to make you stop believing and trusting in the Lord! Satan wants you to quit and give up on the Lord! *DO NOT STOP! KEEP GOING and KEEP FIGHTING TO THE GLORY OF GOD!* When I come to the end of my life's journey, I want to be able to proclaim the words that the Apostle Paul shouted when he finished his work for the Lord! *"I HAVE FOUGHT A GOOD FIGHT, I HAVE FINISHED MY COURSE, I HAVE KEPT THE FAITH: Henceforth there is laid up for me a crown of righteousness, which the Lord, the righteous judge, shall give me at that day: and not to me only, but unto all them also that love his appearing."* (2 Tim 4:7-8) YES LORD! My dear friend, take comfort in knowing that after awhile life's struggles will all be over! Today Jesus is reason enough to keep you fighting in the good fight of faith! A songwriter said the other day, *"When I think of the goodness of Jesus and all that He has done for me, my soul cries out Hallelujah, praise God for saving me!"*

That is my testimony! *It is worth it!* Praise the Lord! Whatever you go through in your life for Jesus, just know that it is worth it! Every sacrifice that you make, and all of the suffering that you may experience in life for the cause of Jesus Christ is worth it! Jesus said, *"Rejoice and be exceedingly glad, for great is your reward in heaven, for so they persecuted the prophets who were before you."* (Matt 5:12 NKJ) It is worth it to me! Every battle that I have in the name of the Lord is worth it! My fasting and praying to get a breakthrough in my life is worth it! It is worth going to Bible study and prayer meetings every week to learn more about my Lord and pray with the Saints of God. My dear friend, sometimes you have to fight to get to the worship services and other church services! Just keep on fighting! *"FIGHT TO WIN!"* That is what the Lord is telling you. Do not just go out and fight to be fighting. *"FIGHT TO WIN!"* The devil is trying to destroy you. *"FIGHT TO WIN" in your marriage! "FIGHT TO WIN" in your home! "FIGHT TO WIN" on your job!* God said, *"Eye hath not seen, nor ear heard, neither have entered into the heart of man, the things which God hath prepared for them that love him."* (1 Cor 2:9) **You must keep fighting so that you will win the prize!**

I am enlisted in the Army of the Lord! I am a volunteer soldier for Jesus Christ! I am a winner and the Word that I share with you is a winning Word! Hallelujah! It is the Gospel of Jesus Christ! You need to know that it does not matter what you fight against. The Word of God assures us that we will be successful against any weapon or foe that we face. Isaiah 54:17 says, *"No weapon formed against you shall prosper, and every tongue which rises against you in judgment, you shall condemn. This is the heritage of the servants of the LORD, and their righteousness is from Me, says the LORD."* (NKJ) *BLESS HIS NAME!* **God said it and that settles it!** The Apostle John encouraged the early church when he said, *"Ye are of God, little children, and have overcome them: because greater is he that is in you, than he that is in the world."* (I Jn 4:4) I share this word of power and deliverance with you to encourage you to believe in the Lord Jesus for everything! Every situation, every trial, and anything that challenges your peace with God are the exact things that God intends for you to war against! *You have the victory!* God wants you to live in the victory of Jesus Christ! The Lord wants you to be delivered and experience the joy and the peace of God in your personal life. *Everything that you need is in Jesus!* *He is the source from which all of your blessings flow!* Jesus speaks expressly to you and offers you this personal invitation to enjoy His victorious life. Revelation 22:17 says, *"And the Spirit and the bride say, Come. And let him that heareth say, Come. And let him that is athirst come. And whosoever will, let him take the water of life freely."*

Sometimes the devil will pick you up and body-slam you. Sometimes he will step on you, trample you and stomp you into the ground. Nevertheless, we can praise the Lord because *God will enable us to rebound! We can get up again!* When the devil thinks that he has killed your spirit, God will give you a pulse and enable you to continue to live! Regardless of what you have gone through, or even may be going through right now, if you have a pulse you are not dead! *God is sustaining your life in spite of your problems!* The Psalmist said, *"Behold, the eye of the LORD is upon them that fear him, upon them that hope in his mercy; To deliver their soul from death, and to keep them alive in famine."* (Psalms 33:18-19) The Saints of God will make it when no body else will! *BY FAITH WE OVERCOME! You are going to make it by faith! Keep on fighting! Do not give up! Do not quit, regardless of what it looks like. KEEP GOING AND KEEP FIGHTING TO THE GLORY OF GOD! YOU HAVE THE VICTORY OVER EVERY SCHEME OF THE DEVIL IN THE MIGHTY NAME OF JESUS!* The Word of God says, *"And we know that all things work together for good to them that love God, to them who are the called according to His purpose."* (Rom 8:28) My dear friend, that scripture is enough to keep you and me fighting and believing to the end!

You may have been ready to give up in some area of your life prior to reading this book or chapter. Give God the reins of your life and allow Him to engineer the changes that are needed to strengthen you and raise you to the *contender* level in Him. You can praise Him because Jesus has given you the victory over the devil today! I challenge you to remember the words of the Apostle Paul that he shared with the Corinthian church, *"But thanks be to God, who gives us the victory through our Lord Jesus Christ. Therefore, my beloved brethren, be steadfast, immovable, always abounding in the work of the Lord, knowing that your labor is not in vain in the Lord."* (1 Cor 15:57-58 NKJ) **It is worth it!** Keep fighting and believing in the Lord. <u>YOU can help somebody if you win a fight</u>! You cannot help anyone if you always quit. In fact, how can you help somebody if you have never had a victory over the devil? How can you encourage anyone to hang on in there and wait for the Lord's deliverance, if you have not been delivered? How can you realistically tell anyone in need that the Lord will carry you through if He has never brought you through? God wants you to know and believe that He is your Savior and the source from whence all of your blessings flow. God is your provider and the sustainer of your life. *The Lord will bring you* *through!* Dismiss, discharge and flush out every tormenting and doubtful thought of the devil. Satan's voice brings fear and confusion. The Prophet Isaiah said of the Lord, *"You will keep him in perfect peace, whose mind is stayed on You, because he trusts in You. Trust in the LORD forever, for in YAH, the LORD, [the Lord Jehovah] is everlasting strength."* (Isa 26:3-4 NKJ) The Lord Jehovah will enable you through the Holy Spirit to be victorious and win your battles against sin and the devil!

My dear friend, the Lord is calling you to a decision in your life. You have to fight, right now, to overcome the negative and doubtful thoughts that Satan is putting in your mind, right now! The devil is trying to knock you out, right now, and shake your faith! He is telling you to try to resolve your problems by yourself a little while longer, or one more time. He knows that you are exhausted and are about to give up. *You must get past that devil and seek the Lord's help!* Regardless of what it is, I encourage you to give it to God. The Lord wants you to be free and to rid yourself of the issues and problems in your life that you have been trying to handle by yourself. God knows that you are tired and have become overwhelmed by them all. Whatever it is that is causing the pain and stripping you of your inner peace, commit that very thing to the Lord by faith, *RIGHT NOW!* It may be the stress of a failed or failing marriage, or family relation. Health issues and financial issues may be taxing your spirit and sapping your strength. Whatever it is, turn it over to the Lord and allow Him to resolve your issues for you. The Apostle Peter said, *"casting all your care upon Him, for He cares for you."* (1 Pet 5:7 NKJ) The world is one big fight! Remember what Jesus said, *"These things I have spoken to you, that in Me you may have peace. In the world you will have tribulation; but be of good cheer, I have overcome the world."* (John 16:33 NKJ) - *"FIGHT TO WIN!"* The devil is trying to put you on the sideline and make you a contestant. Today, God is challenging you to *"FIGHT TO WIN!"* Do not allow the devil to move you from where God wants you to be *in Him! "FIGHT TO WIN!" Today you can be free!*

You can be delivered and you can know that your warring has not been in vain. *The Spirit of the Living God calls you to spiritual warfare as a Christian soldier for Jesus Christ! "FIGHT TO WIN!" - "BE A CONTENDER, NOT JUST A CONTESTANT!"*

Chapter V

ENJOY THE VICTORY!

"For this is the love of God, that we keep His commandments. And His commandments are not burdensome. For whatever is born of God overcomes the world. And this is the victory that has overcome the world, (even) our faith." (I Jn 5:3-4 NKJ)

This is our VICTORY chapter! HALLELUJAH! Everything that has been shared and communicated to this point is designed to bring you to a great climax of total and absolute victory in Jesus Christ! This chapter will focus on challenging you to press on through the storms and battles of life into the victory that God has given to all believers in Christ Jesus! *This is also our JOY chapter!* Everything points to *Jesus Christ* as *the source* of true victory and joy! I want to make this declaration to everyone who reads this book: *I have the victory!* Notice that I did not say that I might have, or hope to have, but I am telling you today that *I have the victory!* Do you? You can answer for yourself after I share my thoughts on the subject.

Victory is the final and complete defeat and the total destruction of an enemy in a military encounter. The soldiers across the globe who have fought in wars know that the reason why you fight is to win. We do not fight to lose. We fight to win! *Victory* is a successful struggle against a legitimate opponent, foe or an obstacle. *Everybody wants to be a winner because winning is fun!* Nobody in his or her right mind likes to lose at anything because there is nothing fun about losing. Did you watch the television coverage of the 2000 Olympics in Sydney Australia? Every day you saw the winners and the losers of each event. In essence, we saw *"the thrill of victory and the agony of defeat!"* The people who got the opportunity to stand on the athletes' victory stand were the people who won first, second or third place in their respective events. They were the people who were *contenders* and not just *contestants!* Similarly, that is what God is trying to tell you and me. *Today, we have the victory because the victory is in Jesus Christ!* I do not know about you, but I am a winner! God put a *winning Spirit* in us because He intends for all of His children to live in the victory of Jesus Christ. The Holy Ghost is a winning Spirit that dwells and abides in the life of every believer in Christ Jesus.

Winners shout in exuberant joy and often make a lot of noise! *Winners* get to participate in post-event interviews. Sometimes winners go overboard and are often penalized in sporting events for what is known as *excessive celebration!* However, the saints of God cannot celebrate the victory that we have in Jesus too much, because nothing can ever match what He did for us to deliver us from our *sin. Jesus is worthy to be praised!* Celebrating the victory of Jesus Christ is the state of being triumphant and victorious in the Spirit of the Lord. *Absolute victory* is what I call it. If you have taken basic math, you have learned that you can get the absolute value of a number or equation. You do this by putting the vertical brackets around the number and declaring the function as being the designator of an absolute value. Consequently, those brackets affect the outcome of the equation or problem; whether the number on the inside is negative or positive. Likewise, *in the Lord,* God is telling us that the *absolute victory* is only possible in Jesus Christ! **Absolute victory is His victory that He gives to us to enjoy!** It is not my victory because I know that I cannot win any battle against the devil on my own strength or merits. It is not your victory because you cannot defeat the devil by yourself! The victory that we enjoy, if we have celebrated anything in the Lord, is only because *JESUS has given us the victory!* That is why the Apostle Paul told the Corinthian church, *"But thanks be to God, WHO GIVES US THE VICTORY through our Lord Jesus Christ."* (1 Cor 15:57 NKJ) This witnesses to the fact that the victory was not yours or mine. The reason you and I can celebrate today is because God has given us the victory *through our Lord Jesus Christ!* Therefore, I can rejoice, shout and praise God today, independent of anyone else's actions or approval, because *JESUS CHRIST has given me the victory! Hallelujah to God!*

Maybe you have never been defeated before in your life. However, I must admit that I have been defeated time after time again. It was not until I became hooked up into Jesus Christ that I really experienced *true victory!* You noticed that I used the term *true victory,* because there are false victories that the devil will permit you to enjoy that are temporary. False victories come and exist for a while until the circumstances or values change in a person's life. A perfect example can be made of the many superstars of past generations that have been long forgotten by the current sports fans and sporting community. Former great athletes in many sports have been all but forgotten. (E.g. Marvin Webster and Jack Sikma of the Seattle Supersonics, and Pistol Pete Marovich of the New Orleans Jazz in basketball; Vida Blue of the Oakland As and Pete Rose in baseball; Billie Jean King in tennis; Joe Capp of the Minnesota Vikings and Hollywood Henderson of the Dallas Cowboys in football; Bullet Bob Hayes who earned the title as the world's fastest human in track and field, to name a few). Superstars compete and are celebrated victoriously as long as they can perform at an exceptional level and win in their respective sporting events. However, as soon as they get a little old, a little slow and weak, the same people who celebrated them over the years will be the ones who kick them to the side and strip them of their value. However, *in the Lord,* it does not matter how young or old you are, you can celebrate the victory in Jesus Christ *as long as you live!* The Bible says, *"I can do all things through Christ who strengthens me."* (Phil 4:13 NKJ) YOU and I have the victory in Jesus Christ over any and everything the devil tries to use to disrupt our fellowship with God. Romans 8.39 says *"nothing shall be able to separate us from the love of God, which is in Christ Jesus our Lord!" Praise His Holy Name!* You can celebrate the victory because you know that *NOTHING* you or anyone else does will change the measure of love your heavenly Father has for

103

YOU! The Apostle Paul said, *"Yet in all these things we are more than conquerors through Him who loved us."* (Rom 8:37 NKJ) In the midst of all these things: our struggles, our failures and distresses, we are *super-conquerors* and *celebrate victory* because God loves us!

Let me share the meat of this lesson with you. There are two things that we all must know to realize *true victory.* I am not talking about this phony stuff that the world gives. I am talking about the victory that comes from the Lord. I trust that you do want to experience *true victory,* the kind that can face the giant Goliath and conquer everything in your path, and work in any situation. If you desire to live in that type of victory, you aspire to be a *contender for Jesus Christ.* First of all, *Spiritual victories are true victories and they come only through obeying the commandments of God.* The proof of our love for God appears in our holy obedience to His Word. We prove our love for God when we obey Him and keep His commandments. That is what our primary scripture is telling us today in 1 John 5.3. The scripture states, *"For this is the love of God..."* In other words, this is what really demonstrates that you love God, *"that we keep His commandments...."* Paul is saying that obedience to the Lord's commandments is how we prove that we love God. Do you really love the Lord today? Paul went on to say, *"And His commandments are not burdensome."* Let me put that in plain talk. God's commandments and rules are not heavy or hard for us to follow. When you really love God, it does not bother you to live like God says to live. When you really love God, you do not have a problem doing what the Lord tells you to do. It is easy. However, if you are straddling the fence and have not made up your mind to fully commit your life to God, then you have problems doing what thus say the Lord. To keep God's commandments is to live in victory! If you ever want to get a victory, just do what God tells you to do. *Obedience,* my dear friend, requires a love for God in your spirit that makes it easy and pleasant to obey His commandments.

You may be asking yourself, *"What does he mean by that?"* Let me explain. Jesus told the scribes and Pharisees, *"These people draw near to Me with their mouth, and honor Me with their lips, but their heart is far from Me."* (Matt 15:8 NKJ) My dear friend, God desires truth and sincerity on the inward part of men. God wants your heart to be right with Him. David, who is considered to be the lover of God, said these words: *"I have chosen the way of truth; your judgments I have laid before me. I cling to Your testimonies; O LORD, do not put me to shame! I will run the course of Your commandments, for You shall enlarge my heart."* (Ps 119:30-32 NKJ) Now let me go over these verses again, more deliberately, so that we can savor the power of the psalmist's words. David said, **"I have chosen the way of truth..."** That portion of the scripture tells us that we all have options in our lives. There are alternatives in our lives that we can choose from. David said, *"I have chosen the way of truth..."* Nobody made him do it. He did it because he wanted to. And today we have choices to make in our personal lives that will make the difference between us experiencing victory or suffering defeat. He went on to say, **"your judgments I have laid before me....."** Now what are judgements? Judgements are decisions. In other words, David said, *your decisions, O Lord, is what I desire and want for my life.* David desired to have the Lord's decisions ruling and governing his life. He continued his profession by saying, **"I cling to Your testimonies; O LORD, do not put me to shame!"** The King James Version says, *"I have STUCK unto thy testimonies: O LORD..."* To stick to something means that you literally have to cling to it, or abide steadfast in a position. In essence, the psalmist said, *"I have stuck to God's words."* What is your position in the Lord? Are you sticking to His word? David went on to say, **"I will run the course of Your commandments, FOR YOU SHALL ENLARGE MY HEART."** The King James Version says, *"I will run the way of thy commandments, WHEN THOU SHALT ENLARGE MY HEART."* The only time any of us will *run the course of God's commandments* is when we fall in love with Him! When you fall

105

in love with the Lord, you will do what He tells you to do! *Glory be to God!*

Think about it in your life. When you fell in love with whomever you fell in love with, all that mattered to you was doing whatever was necessary to please them. Maybe I am the only one who has been in love and did all sorts of crazy things, *in the name of love!* How many crazy things did Kenny Gainous do to try to prove his love to Sharlotte Davison (my high school sweetheart and wonderful wife for over twenty terrific years)? I sent messengers and friends to tell her that I wanted to be with her. I dropped notes off, constantly called her and sent flowers just to try to prove to her that I loved her! *What will you do for love? YOU WILL DO ANYTHING FOR LOVE!* Until you get that love returned, or the response that you desire, you will make a fool out of yourself at times, *all in the name of love.* That is what the psalmist is saying in the scripture. *Lord I will run the way of your commandments....* When will you do it David? *WHEN I FALL IN LOVE WITH YOU!* Are you in love with Jesus today? So the first thing you need to know is *Spiritual victories are true victories and they come only through obeying the commandments of God.*

The second thing you need to know is *Spiritual victories come only through a living and an active faith in the Almighty God.* You must have faith to obey what the Lord tells you to do. I praise God because I know that it is right. *You cannot make it in the Lord without faith!* It takes faith to obey what God tells you to do. At times, God will tell you to do some things that do not make any logical sense! In fact, most of the things God tells people to do will not make any natural sense *or pass the common sense check!* Therefore, if you are ever going to glorify God and celebrate the victory, you must be able to obey the word of God. *Praise His Name!* You have to have faith to obey what God tells you to do. *You will never experience TRUE VICTORY if you cannot believe God.* I John 5.4 says this: *"For whatever is born of God overcomes the world..."* Now what does John mean by this portion of the scripture? He is saying that anyone who is born again conquers the world. The saints of God subdue, prevail and

106

triumph over the world. *And this is the victory that has overcome the world, (even) our faith."*

Now what does that tell us? When I was looking at the scripture, God revealed to me that our spiritual victories come through a constant fellowship and close relationship with God. *The Christians who do not live victoriously are the ones who hit and miss with God!* That means that you are in with God today and you are out with Him tomorrow. *There is no consistency in your walk with the Lord.* The Spirit of Christ is trying to tell all of us that you cannot live in and out with God. *You need to be for Him or against Him!* You may think that you are pleasing both sides. However, the Lord said: *"No one can serve two masters; for either he will hate the one and love the other, or else he will be loyal to the one and despise the other. You cannot serve God and mammon."* (Matt 6:24 NKJ) You cannot have two masters. You must be on fire for one and hate the other.

There is another point I must make at this time. *You cannot live off of the past.* We must keep our relationship with God new and fresh every day. He is not just the God of our fathers. The Lord is not just the God of yesteryears. *He is our Mighty God today!* Yesterday was good, but today is better! *Praise the Lord!* I did not live in the yesteryears, but I am living right now. The songwriter said, *"In times like these we need a Savior!"* *Faith in action gives us the victory over the world!* In other words, you must have *active faith!* Even our little children must demonstrate an active faith to believe that when mommy and daddy tell them to do something, it is for their benefit and their blessing. The adults must have active faith to pursue the goals and dreams in their life. A lot of people talk about it, but how many people actually do it? A lot of people say they believe God, but how many people are really steadfast? Many people say they love the Lord, but how many people are really willing to suffer for God? You cannot just talk about faith and believing! You must come to a point of doing and demonstrating it! *Talk is cheap. It takes spiritual activity to prove that God is real!* The Apostle James said, *"For as the body without the spirit is dead, so faith*

107

without works is dead also." (James 2:26 KJV) Romans 14:23 says, *"whatever is not from faith is sin."* (NKJ) My dear friend, you must know this important truth. *THERE IS NO VICTORY IN SIN!*

Everybody needs to know and understand the impact of sin in any life. The young people and the old alike need to know that there is no victory in sin! Do you know when *you know* that you are defeated? It is when *you feel bad* as a child of God *in your spirit.* God has put a winning spirit in all of us. He is the *Holy Spirit!* Consequently, when you disobey God and discredit your stand for Jesus Christ, you feel sick at your stomach. The sick feeling is a witness to the fact that the Holy Spirit is convicting you of the sin that you are committing. He sounds the *spiritual alarm* in your conscious and lets you know that you are going in the wrong direction. You should be glad today that you are not condemned by your sins because Jesus paid the price for all of us! *Glory be to God!*

Today, there is no victory in sin. The bible says, *"The wages, the results and the compensation for sin is still death. But the gift of God is eternal life through Jesus Christ our Lord."* (Rom. 6.23) *There is life and victory in Jesus!* Our scripture says in I John 5:4, *"For whatever is born of God overcomes the world..."* WHATEVER! I do not care who you are, or how defeated you have been living your life. The bible says, whoever is born of God overcomes and conquers the world! *If you are born of God, you were made to be a winner! "And this is the victory that has overcome the world-- our faith."* Our faith is the cause of victory! Faith, which works by love!

Many people say they are a child of God. Most people in the world believe that they are saved and will go to heaven when they die. However, just because you say that you are saved does not mean that you are saved. Jesus said, *"Not everyone who says to Me, 'Lord, Lord,' shall enter the kingdom of heaven, but he who does the will of My Father in heaven."* (Matt 7:21 NKJ) The evidence of salvation flows through the lives of the believer. The saints of God should not send mixed signals in the world concerning the authenticity of our faith in God. Today, the Lord is reminding the saints of God everywhere to remember that Jesus has given us the victory! *It takes a real Christian, with real faith, to conquer this world!* The world is bad and mean, and poses an insurmountable challenge to natural men. You cannot do it by your self! *It takes the dunamis power of the Living God to conquer the world!*

When you are real, your soul cannot be satisfied with this world. The obstacles that the devil places in your life are there to stop you from believing God. Therefore, you cannot seek your satisfaction in the world. You must seek your satisfaction in God. That is how I can ride around in an old car and be content, because my satisfaction is not fulfilled against the worldly standards of our society. My satisfaction comes from the Lord! *Are YOU seeking to find your satisfaction in the world, or in the Lord?* The Christian revelation enables us to conquer the world, because the revelation gives us faith that reveals the Savior who gives us the victory! ***The victory is only in Jesus, the Author and Finisher of our Faith!***

The devil does not want you to believe or trust God because he knows that *faith brings in the presence of God!* ***THE PRESENCE OF GOD GIVES US THE VICTORY!*** My dear friend, some *Christians* are living defeated lives! They wonder why they are never up, and always seem to be down. You may know someone who is always pining away in grief and never has a positive or encouraging word to share with anyone, *because they are defeated.* They may think that it is a material thing that makes them somebody in the world. However, I want you to know that it has nothing to do with physical possessions and wealth. Everything that is worth anything to God is done in the Spirit of God! The devil does not want you to hear or receive the Word of God because he knows that God is real. The devil also knows that when you praise God, you bring His presence into your life! The psalmist said that the Lord inhabits the praises of His people. That means that the Lord dwells in, sits down and settles Himself in the center of our praise! ***God is enthroned in our praise!*** When we

109

magnify and lift the Lord in our worship services, we bring His power and the awesome glory of God into the place! That's when His blessings begin pouring out on everyone who is in or near the place of worship! Today the saints of God everywhere have the victory over sin and Satan in the mighty name of Jesus!

Countless numbers of Christians are living defeated lives because they have lost their faith and focus in God! Many of us have forgotten who God is and who we are in the Lord! The most important thing to remember is that you are a child of God and He will never leave you or forsake you! It does not matter that you have been making sinful mistakes. You can make mistakes and rebound because the love, mercy and grace of God fill your life. His presence is with us to deliver us and to give us the victory over everything that challenges our peace with God. *Do you have peace in your life?* If you do not have peace, you need to get into the *Spirit of God!* Many saints of God do not have *Joy* because they do not live in the *Spirit of God.* **Carnal Christians** do not enjoy the power of His presence in their life. They look at what the devil is presenting to them and they think that what they see is the end. Nevertheless, you must have enough faith in God to look through the storm, through the blackness of sin, through the obstacles in your way and around the blind curve *by faith* and remember that Jesus said, *"I will never leave you nor forsake you. So we may boldly say: The Lord is my helper; I will not fear. What can man do to me?"* (Heb 13:5-6 NKJ) Jesus said, *"Have faith in God... and, lo, I am with you alway, even unto the end of the world."* (Mk. 11.22 / Matt 28:20)

The devil is a lie today! He does not want the people of God to walk in victory because he knows that victory means power! Today the Lord is saying that we are *super-conquerors!* It does not matter what it looks like. That is what the Lord is saying to you today. Some things in your life might not look right, but you cannot afford to look at them through natural eyes. You must look at them through the eyes of faith! *Faith* says that everything is right, even when it is not right at the present moment! *Faith says that God will always deliver on time, IN ANY SITUATION!*

The Lord commands us to stand still and witness our salvation that He brings in our dilemmas.

My dear friend, you may be discouraged because of past events and disappointments in your life. Today, God says *be encouraged* because He is with you to deliver you in your distresses. ***Take off that yoke that Satan has put on your life!*** The anointing power of God splits the yoke of sin and discouragement that is over your life right now! ***Shake off those shackles that the devil has been using to bind you down! Today, God says that you are delivered!*** You are free and liberated from the burden and the guilt of sin! *YOU HAVE THE VICTORY OVER EVERY SITUATION THAT HAS HELD YOU CAPTIVE! YOU ARE FREE IN THE MIGHTY NAME OF JESUS!* It does not matter how it looks. Today the Lord says *"Rejoice in the Lord, O you righteous: for praise is comely for the upright!"* (Ps. 33.1) *"If God is for you, who can be against you?"* (Rom. 8.31) I want you to say in your heart, *"The devil is a lie!"* Jesus said, *"He was a murderer from the beginning, and does not stand in the truth, because there is no truth in him. When he speaks a lie, he speaks from his own resources, for he is a liar and the father of it."* (John 8:44 NKJ) My dear friend, do not believe the devil's lie concerning your life or future. Regardless of what you are facing in your life right now, ***you are going to make it to the glory of God!*** Keep that thought in your spirit. Expect to receive your blessing from the Lord! ***Expect a miracle!*** *It is a miracle to you and me, but it is nothing to God! He specializes in satisfying the impossible needs in our lives! God's power does not kick-in until your power runs out!* If you can do it, it isn't anything! If you can do it, you do not need God. *God likes the situations where you cannot do it and you acknowledge that you need Him! God glories in the moments when you are standing on His Word and demonstrating faith in Him! He loves to see you waiting on Him to deliver you! God likes the situations where when it is all over, nobody can get the glory but Him! GOD LIKES THE FIERY FURNACES! GOD LIKES THE LIONS' DENS! GOD LIKES THE RED SEAS! GOD LIKES CALVARY! HALLELUJAH!*

111

I have the victory and I am not going to let any devil in hell prevent me from *Enjoying the Victory* in Jesus! It is not in me. It is in the Lord. My dear friend, His presence is with you. That is your reason for hope and faith. Every day that you live you can be assured that His presence is with you. That fact provides you with *God's perfect peace,* in the midst of impossible circumstances. *You are a Contender, not just a contestant!* You have access to all of the resources and heavenly help that God provides His children. Whatever you need, God has it. The psalmist said, *"I will lift up my eyes to the hills-- from whence comes my help? My help comes from the LORD, who made heaven and earth."* (Ps 121:1-2 NKJ) If God can make the heaven and earth, He can handle our little and big problems! Paul said, *"But my God shall supply all your need according to his riches in glory by Christ Jesus."* (Phil 4:19)

You may have been down today, but God says GET UP! Let me close this chapter with these final words of encouragement. It is only through our faith in Jesus and living in the presence of God that we will experience and celebrate *true victory!* Nothing can match the joy and exultation of victory when you have conquered your enemy! *My dear friend, have you had a victory before? Have you ever won at anything that was significant? Do you remember the feeling? Didn't you feel good when you won? What about that time when it looked like you were going to lose and God brought you through?* I remember one of the members of our church fellowship that was on her deathbed and the doctors had basically given her up to die. She walked into the Medical College of Georgia doctors' office with walking pneumonia and ended up in a six-week battle for her life! The doctors had to medically sedate her into a comatose state for her to receive the necessary treatments to combat her illness. It got so bad and doubtful that she would recover, the doctors informed her husband to call her family together because he did not feel that she would get well. However, *the church Prayed and she was healed by the power of God!* God turned her life around and over four years later, she is still with us! *The Lord is able to make a dead situation come alive! Praise His Holy Name!*

I want you to know something my dear friend. There are going to be times when Satan is going to tell you to give up! There are going to be times when he will try to crush you and smoke you like a cheap cigar. Do not be discouraged when the devil is running up and down in your life. God promised you that He would preserve you in the midst of it all! *Hallelujah!* Isaiah 43:1-3 says, *"FEAR NOT, for I have redeemed you; I have called you by your name; YOU ARE MINE. When you pass through the waters, I will be with you; and through the rivers, they shall not overflow you. When you walk through the fire, you shall not be burned, nor shall the flame scorch you. For I am the LORD your God, the Holy One of Israel, your Savior..."* (NKJ) I used this same scripture to support my point in Chapter 4, but I love what it means to us in Chapter 5! *God is the keeper and sustainer of your life and my life!* Therefore, do not be afraid to go through hard trials in your life. Satan wants you to be a timid Christian. He wants you to be a chicken and live in fear of failing. Nevertheless, do not be afraid to go through in your life. The devil wants to destroy you because he knows if you make it through your storm, you will be able to help some other person make it through theirs! If you do not experience the pressures of life and make it, you cannot witness to anyone or strengthen anyone. Never be ashamed to suffer for the cause of Jesus Christ because He was not ashamed to suffer for our salvation! Hebrews 2:9-10 says, *"But we see Jesus, who was made a little lower than the angels, FOR THE SUFFERING OF DEATH crowned with glory and honor, that He, by the grace of God, might taste death for everyone. For it was fitting for Him, for whom are all things and by whom are all things, in bringing many sons to glory, TO MAKE THE CAPTAIN OF THEIR SALVATION PERFECT THROUGH SUFFERINGS."* (NKJ) Do not be ashamed to suffer as a Christian. The Apostle Paul told Timothy " *Yea, and all that will live godly in Christ Jesus shall suffer persecution."* (2 Tim 3:12) The glory of God is revealed in you when you suffer for the cause of Christ. The Bible teaches us that Jesus, the captain of our salvation, was made perfect through His sufferings. When you suffer and make it through the storms of life, you are marked worthy by God and are validated to be a living witness for Jesus Christ. You can witness with certainty of God's ability to deliver His people from the perils of life. Do not worry about your struggles because God said that He would be in there with you! When you cannot do it, God can! Isn't that good news? I have the victory, not because I can, but because GOD CAN! *Praise the Name of the Lord!*

When Israel was in bondage in Egypt, God called Moses to serve as His instrument to bring a great deliverance to His people and lead them into the promise land. Moses did not believe that he could face Pharaoh and successfully lead the children of Israel out of their bondage in Egypt because of his speech impediment. He also remembered that he was a fugitive from the Egyptian penal system because of the previous murder that he committed against the Egyptian centurion. Moses told God that he could not do it because it was humanly impossible for anyone to free such a great multitude of people from a land where they have been trapped in bondage for almost three centuries. The Hebrew people knew no other lifestyle than that of slavery and were reluctant to pursue the offer of freedom, *even if the Almighty God offered the freedom!*

My dear friend, many of us grow accustomed to living in spiritual bondage and reject the offer of true freedom that comes through Jesus Christ our Lord. A person can become so acclimated in an environment of captivity and slavery to sin until they perceive it to be normal. God knew that it was an impossible task for Moses to accomplish Israel's deliverance with his natural strength. However, the Lord God said to Moses *"I have surely seen the oppression of My people who are in Egypt, and have heard their cry because of their taskmasters, for I know their sorrows. SO I HAVE COME DOWN TO DELIVER THEM out of the hand of the Egyptians, and to bring them up from that land to a good and large land, to a land flowing with milk and honey...."* (Exod 3:7-8 NKJ) My dear friend, the Lord your God will come down and give you the victory in the areas of your life that Satan is holding you hostage, even at the very point of death! The Apostle Paul said, *"Yes, we had the sentence of death in ourselves, THAT WE SHOULD NOT TRUST IN OURSELVES BUT IN GOD who raises the dead, who delivered us from so great a death, and does deliver us; in whom we trust that He will still deliver us."* (2 Cor 1:9-10 NKJ) You may not be able to do it, but GOD CAN! That is what the Lord is telling us today. You may be that person that is in bondage. You may be down and out and have been contemplating conceding the fight against the devil and giving up. Today, God says, *"Stand still and see the salvation of the Lord!"* You must know and believe that God is with you. The presence of God brings in His glory and His glory brings the victory in your life today. *Praise the Lord Jehovah!*

God wants you to know that *you already have the victory* through our Lord Jesus Christ! You may think that your situation is impossible, or beyond repair; and *it may be* from a natural perspective. However, I dare you to elevate your thoughts to the *spiritual realm of faith!* When you look through the eyes of faith, you will always see yourself standing on the victory stand and testifying to the glory of God! It does not matter how dark things may look at this moment in your life. It can appear to be as black as midnight, but expect to see the morning and the brightness of the brand new day! David said, *"This is the day the LORD has made; we will rejoice and be glad in it."* (Ps 118:24 NKJ) *"Weeping may endure for a night, but joy comes in the morning."* (Ps 30:5) God has come down to get into the middle of your crisis. The Lord has come down to deliver you from the burden that has taken your joy and placed you into bondage. God has come down to bless you and give you peace in the middle of your storm! You are free to go and live in the victory of Jesus Christ! *Hallelujah!* You may be in a press and struggling beyond measure. *I am speaking to your spirit!* The Lord has come to visit you through these printed words to bring joy where there is sorrow and peace where there has been confusion. Today, the Lord is able to deliver you from any situation that is holding you captive! The Lord Jesus came to set the captives free. He is *your Savior* and the sustainer

115

of your life. You are not running on your fumes, as you are thinking. *God is carrying you through the storm!* You gave out a long time ago, yet He has remained faithful to you. Remember the words of the psalmist, *"Behold, the eye of the LORD is upon them that fear him, upon them that hope in his mercy; TO DELIVER THEIR SOUL FROM DEATH, AND TO KEEP THEM ALIVE IN FAMINE..."* (Ps 33:18-19) My dear friend, the Lord is *your* Keeper, and He is *your* Shepherd! He is the reason that *you* have not been consumed by your troubles!

    TODAY YOUR FAITH GIVES YOU THE VICTORY! *"For whatsoever is born of God overcometh the world: and this is the victory that overcometh the world, EVEN OUR FAITH."* **(I Jn 5:4)** If you are able to come before God and admit that you need the Lord's help in specific areas or situations in your life, He will deliver you and give you the victory. *Your need* may involve your marriage relationship, your home and family, your job, your finances, your health, or a myriad of other things. You may have been trying to handle all of your life's dilemmas by yourself, without success. You may have sought help from other family members or professional people, and you still have the same obstacles facing you. I guarantee that Jesus can satisfy *all your need* according to His riches in glory, *IF YOU BELIEVE! Are you crazy enough to believe Him? Are you crazy enough to trust Him?* If you are, He will bless you! Just try Him! Jesus said, *"With men it is impossible, but not with God: for with God all things are possible. Therefore I say to you, whatever things you ask when you pray, BELIEVE THAT YOU RECEIVE THEM, and you will have them.... if you have faith as a mustard seed, you will say to this mountain, 'Move from here to there,' and it will move; AND NOTHING WILL BE IMPOSSIBLE FOR YOU."* (Mark 10:27 - Mark 11:24 - Matt 17:20 NKJ) My dear friend, *your faith gives you the victory!* Hebrews 11.6 reminds us that demonstrating *faith in God* is the way we actually please Him and inspires God to pour out blessings upon us. We discussed that point in detail in chapter 2. *If you can believe, you can receive!*

116

"For whatsoever is born of God overcometh the world: and this is the victory that overcometh the world, EVEN OUR FAITH." **(I Jn 5:4)** My dear friend, you may be wondering, *"What is the world?"* I will gladly answer. *The world is anything that prevents you from doing the will of God.* You may have been living a defeated life before you read this book. You may have strayed away from the Lord or rejected the will of God. You may have been down in the past because you have not obeyed the commandment of the Lord in your life. Your disobedience may have distanced you from the Lord and caused you to feel abandoned by God. However, right now, the Lord says that you have the victory over everything that has robbed you of your joy and stopped you in your spiritual tracks! Today God has broken Satan's yoke over your life and you are free to *Enjoy the Victory!* You are back in gear and on your way to experiencing a bright future in the Lord! *Praise His Name!* The Bible says, *"But thanks be to God, who gives us the victory through our Lord Jesus Christ."* (1 Cor 15:57 NKJ) How long will you live in bondage? God came down to deliver you and me from the penalty of sin! *Jesus Christ died on Calvary's cross for our sins so that we can be free!*

My dear friend, you must understand that God will get into anything and any situation to give you the victory. **When God shows up, *VICTORY* comes with Him!** That is what He is telling you. God is showing up in your life. He is giving you the victory in your life. Satan is mad, and he is still a lie. God is the blesser and the source from whence all of our blessings flow. You do not need to worry yourself about the conversations of others. People are going to try to convince you that an alternative method and social strategies will satisfy your needs. I encourage you to *stick with God!* If God is for you, who can be against you? *You have the victory over everything!* **Today, the Lord is saying *YES* in your life!** *Healing, deliverance, restoration, strength and power are yours!* Today, God answers the call in your life and satisfies your every need. He looks into your heart and understands your innermost plea. You have hope today in the salvation of God.

117

There is nothing too hard for God! He is able to do it and wants to do it for you! The Lord came to set the captives free, to bring healing and deliverance. Isaiah 53:5 says *"He was wounded for our transgressions, he was bruised for our iniquities: the chastisement of our peace was upon him; and with his stripes we are healed."*

My dear friend, I can hear the voice of Jesus saying *"Fear not...Be not afraid, only believe."* (Mark 5:36) The Lord is speaking these words in your life. ***"Do not be afraid."*** I remember the story of Jesus healing the daughter of one of the rulers of the synagogue named Jairus. The fifth chapter of St. Mark's Gospel gives the account of the events surrounding the healing. Jesus had just healed Legion, the man that was demon possessed, in the land of the Gadarenes. While Jesus walked and ministered to the people in Decapolis, Jairus earnestly begged the Lord to come heal his sick daughter who was at the point of death in his home. When they were enroute to Jairus' house, the woman with the issue of blood detained Jesus with her healing. Jesus looked at the woman and declared that *her faith* made her whole and restored her health. However, the delay was just long enough to prevent Jesus from reaching Jairus' daughter to heal her sickness. The servants from his house came to Jairus in the way and told him not to trouble the Master any more because his daughter had died. Nevertheless, the scripture says, when Jesus heard their words, He looked Jairus in the eye and honored his faith by saying, *"Do not be afraid; only believe."* (Mark 5:36 NKJ) Jesus went to Jairus' house and raised his daughter from the dead! My dear friend, the Lord is telling you today: *do not be afraid.* You, or someone that is dear to you may be suffering health problems and are facing major medical procedures, an operation or some other type of treatment for your ailment, and are afraid. It does not matter what the doctor says, or what the test results may say. It does not matter how bad it looks, or how impossible it may be. Today, God says *fear not!* He has all of the power that you need!

Sometimes it takes a little time to sink in, for you to gather yourself, after receiving bad news. The Apostle Paul reminded Timothy that *"...God hath not given us the spirit of fear; but of power, and of love, and of a sound mind."* (2 Tim 1:7) Likewise, I encourage you to take a deep breath and turn your issue over to God. He can and He will handle it for you. *He is able and willing to satisfy your need.* God wants to do it so that He will be glorified! He wants to show you His power and express His unending love for you. God thrives and magnifies Himself in our moments of distress and adversity. Therefore, the Hebrew writer challenges us to *"...come boldly unto the throne of grace, that we may obtain mercy, and find grace to help in time of need."* (Heb 4:16) Oh yes, *His Grace is sufficient for us and His strength is made perfect in our weakness! Hallelujah to God!*

Let me testify to the glory of God My Savior! I have experienced many victories during the course of my life, in athletic competition and accomplishing personal goals, before and after God saved me! The Lord blessed me to be one of the greatest high school track athletes in the state of Oklahoma when I attended General Dwight D. Eisenhower Senior High School in Lawton, OK between 1975-1978. I won many medals and trophies during my career and was the co-captain of our championship team that won the Oklahoma State Class AAAA championship in 1978. I will never forget that special victory that we experienced when we defeated the defending state champions in the mile-relay, *on the last day of competition, in the last race of the day,* to win the state-championship track meet. *It was a stupendous victory and we celebrated to the max!*

We only qualified five runners to compete in the largest class of high school tracksters. The other powerhouse teams (Edmond, Moore, Tulsa-Washington, Altus, Norman....) qualified from fifteen to twenty-five runners and field event personnel to participate in the state meet. We were clearly at a great disadvantage! However, the Lord blessed us to win, or place, in every event that we competed. *It was a miracle!* When the final race (the mile relay) was about to begin, our coach came to us and

119

told us that we had to beat Norman and Norman had to defeat Edmond, for us to win the state championship. That may seem easy on the surface. *However, history was against us! We had competed against Norman High School for three consecutive years and NEVER had defeated them in the mile relay!* They had the three-time state-champion quarter-mile runner, Jody Jimmerson, to run the anchor leg on their mile-relay team. We had come close to beating them three weekends in a row, before the state meet. Notwithstanding the size of lead that we had over Jimmerson before he got the baton, he always managed to overcome our anchor runner during the last ten yards of the race to give the Norman Tigers the victory. This final race of my high school track career proved to be a race of God's divine favor and my future destiny to become a contender for Jesus Christ!

We ran our hearts out! Every one of us left every ounce of energy and drop of strength that we had out on that track! Don McGee ran the first leg, I ran the second leg, Henry Williams ran the third leg, and Ricky Miller ran the anchor. When Ricky got the baton, he was about five yards ahead of Jimmerson. Everybody *(the sportscasters, coaches, track experts, runners and thousands of spectators)* felt that Jimmerson would pass Ricky, win the race and give Norman the championship! Those of us who had finished our leg of the race lay prostrate on the ground, looking up in sheer exhaustion, to see if Ricky could *somehow* hold him off this one time! Our coach, Coach Carrell Bowman, gave Ricky a new strategy to employ against Jimmerson during this race. He told him to try to make Jimmerson pass him on the curves and force him to run a little longer to get around him. *Ricky did it and it worked like a charm!* When Jimmerson made his last attempt to pass Ricky on the final curve, Ricky appeared to turn on some *invisible jets* and streaked down the final stretch across the finish line, *ten yards ahead of Jimmerson! We instantly got an incredible rush of adrenaline energy and leaped up into the air to celebrate our great victory! Nobody believed we could win the championship with only five runners, BUT US! And that we did!*

120

Oh the joy that filled our souls when they crowned us State Champions!

Let me share another testimony of God's great mercy and grace in my life. I have mentioned throughout the book that I am a soldier in the United States Army Reserves (USAR). I actually served on active duty in the Army for almost eleven years before I entered the USAR. After the Persian Gulf War was over (Operations Desert Shield and Desert Storm), the national government decided to cut the military force significantly and reduce the number of active-duty service members in the Army, Navy, Air Force and Marines. To accomplish this requirement, the military forced thousands of service members to retire early, or exit the military service before they reached the official retirement standard of serving twenty years. The military denied other enlisted personnel the opportunity to re-enlist and continue in the service, if they exceeded a prescribed standard for reaching a specified rank. Officer and enlisted soldier promotion boards were also used to reduce the number of service members in the active military force. If you were not selected for promotion within the prescribed timelines, you were forced to leave and begin a new career in the civilian sector. I will say that the federal government offered nice incentive packages for service members who qualified to receive them, based upon their time in service and Military Occupational Skills (MOS). To make a long story short, I will give you my personal testimony of this seemingly horrible nightmare that more than one hundred thousand service members and their families experienced between 1992 and 1996.

I was one of the officers that *were not selected for promotion* to the rank of Major in the US Army. My promotion board convened in the fall of 1993 and published the results right before Christmas of that same year. *What timing!* Throughout the entire wait, something on the inside of me was letting me know that I was not going to make it, and this was the end of the road for me and my active duty career. *At first, I thought it was the devil and I rebuked the very thought out of my mind.* However, the thought continued to return to me, over and over again, *in my*

121

spirit. I then increased the number of days that I fasted each week and started seeking the Lord for an answer to my worries. I knew that *believers* should remain peaceful throughout any trial, regardless of the circumstances! I remember the many times that I had to convince myself that I would be promoted and would be able to continue my military career in the Army. After all, I had a good file and had done everything that the branch managers suggested to remain competitive with my peers. *I even had a big feather in my hat because I commanded a tactical Signal company during the war and had completed the Command and General Staff College by correspondence! ABOVE THAT, I WAS A CHILD OF GOD THAT WAS LIVING MY LIFE TO GLORIFY HIM!* Therefore, I figured that I was a *sure-shot* for promotion! *NOT!* I have to admit I always felt a little butterfly whenever anyone talked about the promotion-list release date around me. It seemed as though the more I considered not making the promotion list, the bigger the butterflies grew in my stomach. By the time they released the list, I felt as though I had *eagles* flying around in my stomach! They usually call officers who do not make the promotion from Captain to Major *duds!* That means they are not up to par and are not qualified to lead soldiers. I knew I was not a *dud,* but the measure of cuts that were required to satisfy the congressional mandate to reduce the force raised the *dud line* to a higher level! I have some good friends whose branch managers in Washington, D.C. contacted them concerning the Major promotion board. The career managers informed them that they were at risk of not being promoted based upon the competitive strength of their file against their peers, and the limited number of Captains that would be selected at the Major promotion board. The career managers suggested that they should consider submitting paperwork to get out, *take the money and run!* They were excellent soldiers that I would go to war with anytime and anywhere. They were good officers! Many of them distinguished themselves during the Persian Gulf War. Therefore, when it became evident that they would not be around to be considered for promotion, the possibility of me *not making it* was as real as *baseball, hot dogs, apple pie and Chevrolet!*

At that time, I was working in the Studies and Analysis Branch of the Directorate of Combat Developments (DCD) at the United States Army Signal Center in Fort Gordon, GA (Augusta, GA). The Lord had blessed everything that I did on my job and had really established my reputation for producing exceptional work. When the news broke that Captain Kenny Gainous did not make the promotion list to Major, the floodgates opened and a tidal wave of questions and rumors went through DCD like greased lightening! *The inevitable storm had arrived!* I received a telephone call from the director of DCD, Colonel Forrester, informing me that I did not make the list. I had already received the news through the grapevine and had a few hours to consider it before he called. I will never forget the great struggle I had telling my wife, daughter and mother-in-law (who lives with us) that I did not make the list. They were devastated because they felt that I was the best soldier in the world and deserved the promotion. I was glad that they were saved. They knew that the Lord would take care of us, *even if we left the military.* After all, He had taken good care of us *before* we entered the military service! When COL Forrester called, I could feel the pain and disappointment of having to break the news to me through the telephone. He loved me and appreciated the effort and quality of work that I had produced for the directorate throughout my tenure in DCD. I spared him from the dilemma by letting him know that I had received the word earlier and that I accepted the news as God's divine will for me. COL Forrester knew that I was a strong Christian. I encouraged and lifted him by the confidence and determination that I displayed in the face of this adversity. I assured him that I would overcome this challenge in my life and transition out of the military service with *great expectations!* He admired my resolve to accept the news as being my *spiritual permanent change of duty station (PCS) orders from the Lord.* Although I could not believe it was actually happening to me, deep down I knew that the Lord had made this decision for my family and me. *My calling into a new dimension of Gospel Ministry was the bottom line for everything that I had experienced and the reason why I had to get out!* I had an unction and intuition that it was true then. *I am absolutely sure about it now!*

I actually had another opportunity to go through a subsequent promotion board before I had to get out of the active component. My superiors had even encouraged me to stay in and were willing to ensure that I worked in a position that would increase my chances for promotion during the ensuing board that would convene the following year. However, I prayed for guidance in making the decisions for my future and the Lord moved me to get out without going through another board. Chances are much slimmer at the next board anyway. Regardless of the chances, I made my mind up to get out and they scheduled me to depart active military service on 1 June 1994. Now all of the *drama* surrounding my transition from the military to civilian life began.

The very first thing I had to do was decide where we would live and what job I could work so that I could adequately provide for the family. I had been in the military since I graduated from college and never interviewed or put a resume together for job solicitation. In fact, I did not know where to begin looking for work, except around the military environment. I will never forget that night that I really sought God's direction concerning where I should reside and what He wanted me to do in ministry. It was approximately three days after I had received the news about the promotion board results. My pastor, Bishop F.D. Lawson, Jr., always taught me to *keep dirty knees (meaning pray constantly), study your Word (the Bible) and trust God (have faith).* Those lessons became more real to me at that moment of my life than I could imagine. I remembered what the Lord had already done for my family and me over the years. Psalms 34:19 and Psalms 37.25 began to ring in my spirit to bring peace in my life. David said, *"Many are the afflictions of the righteous, but the LORD delivers him out of them all." "I have been young, and now am old; yet I have not seen the righteous forsaken, nor his descendants begging bread."* (NKJ) That was my answer! The Lord would reveal His divine plan for me and I would obey it by faith!

That night I prayed diligently for the Lord to reveal His will to me. I remember getting off my knees and getting into bed with a calm assurance that I would hear from the Lord. *Never would I have imagined that it would be that same night!* The Lord spoke to me that night in a most profound way. At first, I did not know that the Lord was speaking to me. I thought that Sharlotte was trying to get me to turn over so that I would stop *snoring!* Then I realized that the voice was not Sharlotte's, but the Lord's. I heard His voice telling me to remain in Augusta, Georgia. *I could not believe my ears!* I am a mechanical design engineer by degree and I could not imagine finding any work in that field in the Augusta, GA area. Despite my uncertainty concerning work, I knew in my heart that I had heard from the Lord. The Lord then revealed to me that He would establish a ministry through me in Augusta that would transform the lives of men. He even allowed me to see a portion of the ministry in a vision that same night. *What a mighty God we serve!* That is all I needed to know: where to go and what to do! My path was set and I was implementing the Lord's plan immediately!

The next morning I got up and called Sharlotte into room so that we could pray. I shared with her the Lord's directions concerning our family and my ministry and informed her that Augusta, Georgia would be our permanent home. She willingly accepted the news and we immediately began our transitional planning to stay in the Augusta area. We had always lived in government housing throughout my military career and had never owned our own home before. This was a tremendous challenge for us. Naturally, I could stay anywhere as long as my family was happy. It would be our home, but it would certainly have to satisfy *Sharlotte's* wonderful taste. To make a long story short, the house-hunting ordeal proved to be a *small nightmare!* It became burdensome and tormenting at times. I cannot begin to tell you the number of houses that we looked at, or the different decors that we had to remember during the process. After much pain and suffering, we realized that no existing home contained everything that we wanted. Consequently, our realtor recommended a builder to us and we decided to build a house to our own specifications. This was not supposed to be our dream house, but it certainly had to be comfortable. I modified a nice floor plan that the builder showed us to suit our needs and we were on the way! *WITHOUT A JOB!*

The Lord told us to stay in Augusta. *Based upon His word,* we had faith enough to begin building a house in January that would be finished in May so that we could move in before I left the Army. *I did not have a clue as to where I was going to work when I got out of the service.* It was not a problem at the time because I was still in the Army and would continue to receive a paycheck until 1 June 1994. The realtor wanted them to begin the work immediately to increase the probability that the builder could finish the house before I got out of the military. This would ensure that we would not have any problems closing on the house in the event that I did not have a civilian job secured by June 1. February came and went and I had not landed a job. I had started interviewing with several military recruiters for large industry firms that sought to hire officers leaving the active force. Several latched onto me because I possessed a technical degree and promised me that I would excel in the civilian workforce because of my degree and military experience. *The only problem that I had was location.* I constantly reminded them that I was limited to the Augusta, GA area! Many opportunities opened for me to accept excellent jobs in other cities and states, but I had to turn them down. *The Lord said stay in Augusta and that is what we were going to do!* Well, March passed and I still did not have a job. Sharlotte started picking her colors and ordered all of the things that would go into the house. I picked the brick and the trim. *STILL NO JOB!* Some of my friends started passing by the house and saw the progress the builders made. They would ask me about my future employment and I would report, *"nothing on the radar screen yet!"* I could read their minds, *"YOU FOOL!"* One of my good friends at work could not believe that I was building a house without knowing where I was going to work. *He called me a fool to my face and laughed about the whole thing! He just knew that I was joking, until he actually visited the building site with me. THEN HE GOT SICK!* He recommended that we stop the building process, get an apartment or something less binding and stay there in the event that I could not find work in the area. I shared with him that the Lord instructed me to stay in Augusta to start my ministry and that was what we would do. Besides, we would have faced legal ramifications if we had quit the building process at that point. *We were committed and could not turn back now!* Of course, it did not make any sense to him because he was not a believer. However, it made perfect sense to me because I knew what the Lord told me to do. *I was acting on my faith and standing on the word of God! He said it and I did it! It was up to God to provide me a job!*

April came, went, and still no job! The builders were starting to put bricks on the structure and put the interior walls and details in. I have to admit I started getting a little anxious by then. I received several calls from the military recruiters offering me big money to take jobs all across the nation. I simply told them *"No. If it ain't Augusta, I can't take it!"* They could not believe that anyone would reject some of the offers that they presented to me. By then, it was the end of May and I settled on doing any job that would pay the bills so long as it was in the area. I really started praying that the Lord would provide me an opportunity to work in the area, or show me where to look for a job. Compounding the problem was the fact that we experienced several weeks of bad weather during the middle of April and the first part of May. The bad weather delayed the builder's progress in completing the house in May and cancelled our hopes for closing on the house before the 1 June 1994 target date that I was scheduled to depart the active Army. The delay actually pushed our closing date back from the end of May to 20 June and jeopardized our ability to close on the house because I changed employment. This was a nightmare unfolding before all of our eyes: the builder, the realtor, the financial agency, the lawyer and my family. However, all of us discovered that *God specializes in situations like these!*

127

Just when I started losing hope for obtaining a good and fulfilling job, Mr. Dwayne O. Fulton, Technical Director for Information Technology Solutions, Inc. (ITS, Inc.) at the Fort Gordon Battle Lab, approached me and offered me a job. Unknowingly to me, he had been watching me and inquiring about my performance as an Operations Research analyst for the government. Mr. Fulton read several of my technical studies that I completed for DCD. He knew that I possessed engineering and analytical skills that could benefit his organization. Mr. Fulton told me that he had heard that I was leaving the active force and was looking for employment. He also said that he had a limited budget that would not permit him to pay me all that he felt I deserved. However, he promised me that he would adjust his future contracts to ensure that he compensated me at the appropriate level, if I accepted the offer. He also knew that I was a Gospel minister and assured me that he would support whatever requirements I had in the ministry. *THAT WAS AN EYE OPENER and an essential factor in my decision!* Additionally, he was a Major in the USAR and offered to help me get into the reserves so that I would be able to gain a supplemental income through the USAR. In fact, he made the call for me to contact the approving authority to place me in a brand new reserve unit that was activating in Atlanta, GA and moving to Fort Gordon, GA (Augusta, GA) that summer! *This was incredible*! To put the icing on the cake, the one person who could authorize my acceptance into the USAR in the area was an officer that I had served with on active duty eleven years earlier! He and I served together in the 3-18th Field Artillery Battalion at Fort Sill, Oklahoma. I remembered him and he remembered me. He instantly put me into the new unit and my reserve career had begun one week before I departed active duty! *Nobody but God could do something like that!* That is not all, COL Forrester was informed that four Government Services (GS) positions were being created in the DCD and he wanted me to pick the one I wanted, and fill it. It paid almost eight thousand dollars more than the offer I received from Mr. Fulton. When Mr. Fulton heard about my government offer, he told me to pray over it and let him know what my decision was. That is exactly what I did. I prayed and the Lord told me to accept the position with Mr. Fulton and *He* would provide the rest! I informed him of my decision to accept his offer with ITS and that was the beginning of a life-long relationship with him. He has truly been a man of his word and has exceeded his promise to compensate me for making that initial sacrifice to accept a reduced salary to get me in the door. *God is good, all the time!* By the way, the post eventually eliminated those GS jobs due to Reduction in Force (RIF) requirements. That would have been me, if I only made my decision for accepting the jobs based upon the quantity of money. *Thank God for prayer and faith!*

Everything seemed to be falling into place now. *The Lord* wired my *faithless hecklers'* mouths shut concerning my *building the house without a job decision!* However, I still faced the seemingly insurmountable closing issue. The builder completed the house on June 19, 1994 and it was beautiful! Unfortunately, it may have been for naught if the finance agency was unwilling to risk funding our loan since I recently changed my employment and was no longer in the active Army. It was so shaky at the closing that my realtor did not have confidence that we could successfully close on the house if I revealed that I was no longer on active duty. The lawyer had my wife and I complete a stack of closing papers for the house. One of the documents specifically asked me a question concerning my employment with the military. The devil told me to answer that I was still in the Army, although I knew that I was not. Satan tried to get me to rationalize the question by suggesting that my employment in the United States Army Reserves was the same as being on active duty. I knew that was deceptive and untrue. However, all I could do was think of the great disappointment my wife and family would suffer if we did not close on the house that day, not to mention the embarrassment! It was overwhelming to me, and I figured that what they *[the lawyer and finance agency]* did not know would not hurt any of us! *Boy was I wrong!* We successfully closed on the house. The lawyer completed all of the checks, handed the ones out to the people who were due them that were present, and put the rest in the mail. We all hugged, shook hands and departed with big smiles on our faces. The ride across town was an absolute nightmare to me. *I compromised my spiritual integrity with the Lord and was now the ultimate loser! I knew that I lied and failed to trust God in this situation.* In spite of all that He had proven to us over the past four months, I did not trust Him to deliver us in this situation. *I was sick and Sharlotte was sick too.* She did not say anything because she just knew that I would. I believe she was in shock by my actions! Nevertheless, *my spirit* could not rest within me. Conviction and shame took an enormous toll on me. Within one hour of leaving the lawyers office, I called back to inform him that I had answered the employment question incorrectly and that I was no longer on active duty, but in the reserves. He shouted in horror because he stated that the closing was invalid and he had already mailed the remaining checks. *I thought that I was going to jail that night!*

My mother-in-law and daughter had already loaded up her car and had started moving some of their smaller things into the house. We told Mom that we might not be able to move into the house as planned because of some legal issues. She said OK *and continued to move her things into the house! She was not going to be denied, or delayed, and Ebony (our eleven year-old daughter at that time) followed her lead!* We had scheduled the movers to pick up our furniture and move all of it over to the new house the next day. *You are talking about a mess! That is what sin is: ONE BIG MESS!* After the lawyer gathered himself, he realized that there was still hope for restructuring the closing, if I had a job and the job involved performing the same duties that I did in my previous job in the military. *Praise God it did!* He sighed in great relief and told me to stand by while he contacted the finance agency. I asked him if I needed to cancel my moving appointment and he said no, not yet. *Sharlotte and I also sighed in great relief!* As soon as we ended the telephone call with the lawyer, Sharlotte and I got down on our knees *and I asked the Lord to forgive me* for not trusting Him to deliver us at the closing. I then asked the Lord

130

to fix the whole mess for us and permit us to close legally with our current status and job information. We got up and waited with expectation that the Lord would work *one more miracle* for us, *and that He did!* The telephone rang about thirty minutes later. It was the lady from the finance agency! She informed me that the lawyer had explained the whole situation to her. She then asked me to provide her some information concerning my employment so that she could determine if we could simply reschedule another closing to complete the corrected paperwork. She asked me if I could get a letter from my employer stating my salary and duty description, and most importantly, could I provide a copy of a pay stub reflecting that I am employed and receiving pay? I answered yes to all and had my boss draft up the official letter from our company. I had only been working for ITS for three weeks and had received *ONE* pay check and *ONE* pay stub to verify my pay! *You talking about an Awesome God moving on behalf of a pathetic person, IT WAS ME!* With all of the finance agency's requirements satisfied, they rescheduled our closing for the next day!

Before the finance representative ended her conversation with me, she stated that she would not have ever imagined that anyone would call to correct a deliberate mistake in the manner that I did. She went on to say that she has never seen any act of honesty in the magnitude that I displayed that day, *especially when it clearly jeopardized everything that I hoped to gain and enjoy.* She then concluded our conversation by saying these words, *"Captain Gainous, you must truly be a man of God and a man of great integrity. If you can be this honest in a matter of this magnitude, with everything on the line, you certainly are the type of client that we seek to gain in our business. I will see you tomorrow at the closing and I pray that your wife, your family and you will enjoy that beautiful house."* Never would I have imagined that anyone with knowledge of my failure would be able to see anything *positive* in my character. *Her words healed me.* The next day, all of us reassembled at the lawyer's office to re-sign all of the new paperwork. Before we got started, I asked everyone in the room to forgive me for my sin and the extra work that they had to

131

do as a result of my poor judgement. Everybody was happy that I did correct my mistake and were pleased that everything worked out for all of us. With that, Sharlotte and I signed all of the paperwork and departed new homeowners! *This time with the Lord's blessings and grace upon us!* When Sharlotte and I left that lawyer's office on June 21, 1994, we were filled with joy and thankfulness to God for all He did for us to free us from the burden of my sin. *Nobody but the Lord can snatch victory out of the jaws of defeat as He did for us that day! God gave us the victory!* That experience and victory gave me a renewed determination to fulfill my purpose in the Lord. It also taught me the value of walking in the truth and integrity of the Lord. I really came to know that I must *trust Him* in every situation.

Those were two great moments of victory in my life. However, nothing can compare with the victory the Lord gave Sharlotte and me during her pregnancy with our daughter Ebony. My wife and I decided to have a baby during my senior year in college. I know today that it was God's divine plan for us to have the baby before I finished school. The Lord had put it in Sharlotte's spirit and confirmed it in mine. So five months after we were married, Sharlotte conceived and we became expectant parents! We praised God when we received the news that Sharlotte was pregnant. Everything was going well and I enjoyed watching Sharlotte grow month after month. She seemed to become more beautiful to me as the months went by. The thought of having a baby and raising a child overwhelmed me. The bible says, *"Behold, children are a heritage from the LORD, the fruit of the womb is a reward. Like arrows in the hand of a warrior, so are the children of one's youth. Happy is the man who has his quiver full of them; they shall not be ashamed, but shall speak with their enemies in the gate."* (Ps 127:3-5 NKJ) I believed every word of that scripture and could not wait for the baby to arrive!

Sharlotte was also my high school sweetheart and had always been very healthy and active to that point. She was deeply involved in church activities and played the flute in the Eisenhower High School marching and concert bands. She never suffered any significant illness, except for the time she caught the *chicken pox* when she was a junior in high school. *Can you believe that? I couldn't!* Besides that, she was as healthy as a lark! The first five months of her pregnancy went as smooth as ice and were very enjoyable. However, I have to admit that I was shocked by some of her newly acquired tastes and cravings for strange food combinations like *Cracker Jacks with Nacho Cheese Doritos!* Nonetheless, both of us were enjoying watching the life of our child grow within her throughout the pregnancy.

One day Sharlotte began feeling sharp pains in her left foot. She was about six months pregnant at the time and we felt that the added weight that she had gained over the first five months of the pregnancy was causing the pain. However, the pain increased over the next five days and reached an unbearable level for her. She worked for Oklahoma State University and had excellent medical insurance, so I took her to the doctor to see if he or she could determine the cause of her foot problem. The doctor x-rayed the foot and decided that it was a simple muscle pull that would heel itself in a week or so, if she stayed off it. *What a relief!* The doctor gave Sharlotte some crutches and an orthopedic shoe to wear until it healed. Consequently, the pain in her foot increased and the crutches caused her wrists to swell and inflame when she used them. This alerted us and we began to sense that this was not a simple ailment that would heal itself, or go away in a short time. In fact, more symptoms began to surface and she began to experience acute pain in both her feet and wrists. Subsequently, her hair started falling out and she began to lose weight rapidly. *I could not believe my eyes!* It was as though I was living a nightmare! I literally watched the devil afflict my wife, *with God only knew what,* and I could not do a thing about it, *but pray and trust God for the healing!*

Sharlotte's boss at the University Computer Center was Dr. Robert Gumm. He was a devout Christian that loved Sharlotte dearly. He passed several years ago and has gone on to be with the Lord. Dr. Gumm hired Sharlotte on the spot, the very first day he saw her during the job interview. He hired her to be the University

Computer Center's staff secretary. Dr. Gumm was truly a blessing to both of us. He knew that I was in school and Sharlotte was providing the bulk of our income for the family. I will never forget the day that Dr. Gumm called me to come get Sharlotte from work because she had suddenly become extremely sick and could not walk. I was alarmed and immediately ran over to her job to check on her. Dr. Gumm told me that he wanted me to take her to the hospital to see a specialist and keep her there until she was well. He then told me not to worry about her job or finances because he would pay her complete salary as long as she would get proper medical attention. *That was pure love in the highest order!* He and everybody at the Computer Center truly demonstrated their love for Sharlotte and prayed that she would get better. Nobody knew what was causing her sickness. It took all of us by surprise!

Sharlotte's little sisters (Trocha, Rocha (twins) and Chee Chee (Sheril)) were visiting us at the time and were devastated by all that was going on with her failing health. They were about ten or eleven years old and were scared and confused by all that was happening to her. One evening I called from work to check on them. Chee Chee answered the telephone in an alarming way and I could hear the girls crying in the background. When I asked what was going on, she told me that Sharlotte was experiencing *nerve-racking pain* in her hands and feet that left her paralyzed on the couch. When I got home and saw her condition, I could not do anything but cry out to my God for help! I called L.P. Williams (my best friend and fellow minister of the Gospel of Jesus Christ) and his wife (Arnetta) to come over so that we could anoint Sharlotte and pray for her healing. *We anointed her in the name of the Lord and prayed the prayer of faith!* The Lord touched Sharlotte and allowed her to sleep well that night. We were very grateful. From that moment, Arnetta prepared dinner for Sharlotte and me three or four times a week, to relieve her from that duty and *to keep me from looking like Wile E. Coyote!* Fried-chicken, baked beans and potato salad! That was her specialty and it was delicious!

134

As the days passed, Sharlotte's health began to deteriorate rapidly. Her doctor decided to send her to the bone and joint specialist in Oklahoma City, OK (OKC) to see if they could determine the cause of her joint condition. Sharlotte's parents and my parents came to Stillwater to see her before the doctor admitted her to the Bone and Joint Hospital in OKC. I will never forget the pain and grief, the weeping and moaning, and the heart-rending prayers to God that occurred in our married student-housing apartment that day. I can still see Sharlotte's father, a great big man, Mr. Roy T. Davison, kneeling down before her, bathing her feet with his own tears while he cried out to God for His mercy. I remember looking into my mother-in-law's eyes and seeing the confusion and shock in them when she saw Sharlotte's horrible health condition. The entire ordeal riveted my parents to the couch and left them stunned. Consequently, I felt like an absolute failure as a husband. *Yet we prayed and trusted God for her deliverance!*

I had already received my commission as a second lieutenant in the United States Army Reserves, and was just waiting to graduate from OSU so that I could begin my active duty career in the Army. My dad was an old soldier in the Army and knew the free medical benefits and hospital care that Sharlotte would receive when I entered active duty. On a trip to the store during their visit, my dad asked me had I considered going on active duty early because of Sharlotte's medical condition. He even assured me that the Army would allow me the time to finish my degree, and pay for my classes, if I decided to go in early. My dad did not force me to do it or make me feel uncomfortable during the conversation. I knew that he spoke out of his sincere love and concern for Sharlotte and me. I also knew that it would be the best thing for me to do, *from a natural perspective.* My dad has never given me any bad advice to date in my life. However, on that dark summer day in Oklahoma, I did not do what he suggested. Something on the inside of me, *the Spirit of the Living God,* told me to stay in school and trust God to deliver us from this horrible experience. After hearing everything that my dad shared with me concerning going into the Army early, I looked my dad in

135

his eyes and told him that I am going to stay in school. I shared with him that I was totally depending on God to heal Sharlotte and deliver a healthy baby. I told him that God did not bring us this far to forsake us. I also told him that I had to finish my education now, *in the middle of the storm,* or I would not finish at all. ***That statement of faith changed my life forever!***

I must share this information to enlighten you of my *faith-building* experience with God. During Christmastime in 1980, *the Lord opened time and the future for me.* God allowed me to see Ebony born in the hospital, lying in Sharlotte's arms, over a year and ten months before she was actually born (October 13, 1982). In that vision, I saw myself standing in the doorway of the recovery room in the hospital looking in at Sharlotte and Ebony as they were lying in the bed. I also saw a figure of an older man dressed in a black suit standing in the doorway beside me. I did not see his face and did not know who he was at the time. When the Lord gave me the vision, I thought the vision was my assurance that Sharlotte and I would stay together and get married. *[Sharlotte caught me red-handed doing some unacceptable things when we were dating, and was contemplating breaking up with me! I repented and asked the Lord to save our relationship and bless me to marry Sharlotte. God heard my prayer and kept us together. Things got R-E-A-L SHAKY there for a while, but the Lord brought us through! Today, over twenty-one years later, I can praise the Lord because we have been happily married for over twenty wonderful years!]* The night I saw the vision, it was so crystal-clear and real that I actually felt it had happened! I woke up the next morning and realized that it was a divine revelation from God. I never forgot the vision and I kept it in my heart and spirit. I did not share it with Sharlotte or anyone. Although I was a baby Christian at the time, I knew that God gave me the vision for a *special purpose.* Never would I have imagined that it would be the source of my spiritual strength and hope for God's mercy and deliverance during Sharlotte's illness. The revelation gave me the *faith* that I needed to make it through the enormous storm that we faced during Sharlotte's sickness and affliction.

Dr. Jon D. Blascky, one of the most qualified bone and joint doctors in the state of Oklahoma, took Sharlotte as his patient. He ran a series of tests on her to determine the origin of her acute joint pain and the cause of the inflammation in her feet and wrists. I was in summer school at the time and was taking ten hours of engineering and technology courses. Oklahoma City was an hour drive from Oklahoma State University. L.P. and I traveled four or five times a week, over a three-week period, to visit Sharlotte while she was in the hospital. That was truly a heartbreaking experience for me. I will never forget the first time that Dr. Blascky shared his diagnosis and prognosis of Sharlotte's condition with me. Almost two complete weeks had passed before they could make a legitimate call on her condition. He informed me that Sharlotte had a very serious and potentially deadly disease, *Lupus.* He went on to tell me that the disease attacks the major organs (liver, lungs, kidneys etc.), the joints and destroys the red blood cells in the body. He told me that it was active in her and could cause severe complications in Sharlotte's pregnancy that could cause her to lose the baby. *I did not EVEN want to hear that!* He continued by saying that, if the baby survived the pregnancy, she would probably be severely retarded or she would suffer some sort of serious birth defect. *Now you know I could not take that, even from the expert!* I openly rebuked the thought and began to share with him my faith in God! I told Dr. Blascky that I was a *Believer* and I would not accept anything negative that he told me about Sharlotte's condition or the baby's health. I informed him that God was a healer and He would deliver Sharlotte and the baby from death and destruction! He looked at me and said these words, *"I know that you are religious and I can appreciate that. However, you do not know what you are up against, this disease is very serious and it can be a killer. Your wife is in very serious condition and the baby's health is certainly at risk."* I looked at Dr. Blascky with tears in my eyes and declared to him that *MY GOD* will make the difference in it all! I told him to do all that he could for Sharlotte and God would do the rest. He looked at me with amazement and left the room. L.P. and I went in, had prayer with Sharlotte and rode back to Stillwater together, conversing about the doctor's words.

The next day, the Lord led me to begin fasting and praying for Sharlotte. I shared the news with L.P. and he decided to join me in a three-day fast for her healing. I realized that prayer alone would not satisfy my need in this situation. The words that Jesus spoke to His disciples in Matthew 17:21 kept ringing in my ears. Jesus said to His disciples, *"However, this kind does not go out except by prayer and fasting."* (NKJ). That was my answer: *fasting and prayer! I was convinced that those two ingredients, combined with my unwavering faith in God, would give us the victory!*

I was in the middle of final's week and could not get over to see Sharlotte for three days. It had been three weeks since I had seen her walk. She had been totally bed-ridden up to the time L.P. and I began our fast. In fact, Sharlotte's natural weight, without being pregnant, is between 110 and 113 pounds. *[She is only 5'-2" tall, if you are stretching her! She claims that she is 5'-2 ½"]* At the time she was in the Bone and Joint Hospital in OKC, she had lost down to 104 pounds, at six months pregnant! *She was a pitiful sight.* She had gotten so small that she had to tell the x-ray technicians she was six months pregnant and that she could not take an x-ray. They did not believe her until they reviewed her medical records. Over the first two weeks that L.P. and I visited her in the hospital, she continually lost weight. I was very concerned, and that is when the Lord led me to fast.

I will never forget that day that L.P. and I completed our fast and visited Sharlotte in the hospital. Something told me that I would witness the power of God during the fast. We traveled over to the hospital and went in to see Sharlotte in her room. We usually timed our visits so that we would be there when Dr. Blascky would make his daily round to check on Sharlotte. On that particular day, he had not visited her yet. Every day that I would see Sharlotte I would ask her how she felt and how much did she weigh. Up to that point, it was bad news, discouraging news or no news. She was always in pain and always had lost some more weight, all the way down to 104 pounds. However, *on this particular day,* I asked her how she felt and she said that she felt great and that the Lord had given her relief from much of the pain over the past several days. *[The exact days that we had been fasting!]* I then asked her how much she weighed. She responded by saying 104.5 pounds! *That was a half-pound more than the last time we saw her! I leaped on my feet and began praising God all over her hospital room! I started shouting, "SHE IS HEALED! SHE IS ON HER WAY BACK! PRAISE GOD!"* The people in the hospital came to see what the ruckus was about. When they saw me, I had *tears of joy* in my eyes and *the hope of God* in my heart! *That wasn't all!* After I settled down, Sharlotte told me that she wanted to show me something. She then moved the covers back on her bed, pulled her legs over the edge, stood up *[unassisted]* on her own two feet *and walked across the room praising the Lord! I WAS FIT TO BE TIED! OH THE JOY THAT FLOODED MY SOUL! TO GOD BE THE GLORY!* By the time Dr. Blascky arrived, we already had conducted a church service in her room! It was something to behold. It had been three weeks since I saw Sharlotte walk and that was something special to me. The doctor joined in the celebration and eventually released Sharlotte to return to Stillwater after three days. *I want you to know that fasting and prayer will work miracles for you!*

Within three weeks, Sharlotte gained ten pounds and began functioning at a normal level again. It was September then and the baby was due to be born in October. Everything seemed to be going well. Then the devil started another *drama episode* during the final two weeks of Sharlotte's pregnancy. L.P. and I were taking an Old Testament class for an elective that semester. On one occasion, we were in class and heard a knock at the classroom door. Our teacher went to the door and opened it. When the door opened, I could see that Sandra Richardson *[a strong sister in our Bible Study and Church Fellowship]* was standing at the door. I immediately knew that it had to be something that involved L.P. or me. I took a closer look and could see that Sandra was crying. She was trying to explain to the professor that she needed to see me right then and that it could not wait until class was over. At that moment, L.P. and I got up and went out in the hall to see what was going on. Sister Sandra informed me that she had taken Sharlotte in for one of her scheduled pre-natal doctor's appointments and the doctor could not find or hear the baby's heartbeat. She said they immediately admitted Sharlotte into the hospital to run tests and see if the baby had died in her womb. She began to weep and cry in my arms. Everyone in our church fellowship knew all that Sharlotte and I had experienced over the past two months with the pregnancy. She and every member of our Bible Study had been fasting and praying that Sharlotte would have good health the remainder of the pregnancy. *Now look what the devil was trying to do to us! He was trying to kill our unborn baby!* I held Sandra in my arms and told her not to worry because the Lord would surely deliver. I declared my faith in God by saying, *"Brother and sister, I do not know why the doctor cannot hear the heartbeat, but it is still there! He just cannot hear it! I do not know what has happened but I know that the baby is going to be fine!"* I was holding on to the dream and vision that God had given me of Ebony being born in the hospital almost two years before. *I embraced that vision and gripped it as if it was the Lord Himself!* I refused to accept anything but good news! *I spoke my daughter's life into existence BY FAITH!*

Sandra pulled her car around, picked us up and drove us to the Stillwater Medical Center where they had admitted Sharlotte. L.P. and I prayed all the way over to the hospital. I remember asking the Lord to heal the condition and allow the baby's heartbeat to start registering on the monitor when I get to the room. I prayed and prayed for God's mercy and grace over Sharlotte and the baby. When we arrived at the hospital, L.P., Sandra and I boarded an elevator and started up to Sharlotte's room. Before the door opened, I said one more short prayer, *"Lord please let the baby's heart function properly and allow me to see the evidence of the baby's heartbeat when I get off of this elevator and enter the room."* That was my prayer and that is exactly what the Lord did! I got off the elevator and ran to Sharlotte's room. When I arrived at her door, I peered in and saw the biggest smile in the world on Sharlotte's face! Her beautiful dimples were making the smile much more profound and her eyes were beaming with tears of joy! *God had delivered again!* I walked into the room and heard the baby's heartbeat monitor broadcasting and proclaiming the sounds of Ebony's life. The computer printout registered a strong and regular heartbeat! *I don't know how He did it, but I thank God that He did! Another episode, another victory to the Glory of God!* We were all relieved and exhausted by the ordeal. We were only two weeks out from Sharlotte's due-date and wondered what would Satan try next to stop our child from being born.

Well, two days before her due-date, Sharlotte had another pre-natal appointment with her doctor. During that visit, the doctor discovered that Sharlotte's placenta had begun to deteriorate and had reached a very dangerous level. Her doctor, Dr. Lyles, felt that the baby was at risk and was not receiving the proper nutrients to ensure good health and a safe delivery. Sharlotte had been required to take several medications to combat her lupus problems. Dr. Lyles felt that the medications contributed to the degradation and decaying condition of her placenta. Sharlotte was at full-term pregnancy and could deliver at any time. She had started experiencing some mild contractions and labor pains, but nothing severe. After running more tests on the placenta and the baby, he concluded that Sharlotte's health and the baby's health were threatened. Dr. Lyle called us into his office and informed us of his concerns, the test results and the risks that were involved with delaying the baby's delivery. He had a great concern that Sharlotte's weakened physical condition and the trauma that accompanies a natural childbirth would jeopardize the life and safety of Sharlotte and the baby. Therefore, he recommended that Sharlotte undergo a Caesarian section to deliver the baby. After all that we had experienced over the past three months, *that was good news!* Dr. Lyles scheduled the surgery for Wednesday at 10:00 am, on October 13, 1982.

We checked Sharlotte into the hospital on Tuesday evening. We were extremely excited and took pictures of Sharlotte as we left our married student-housing apartment to go to the hospital. The nurses checked her in and told her to get a good night sleep. Naturally, we could not sleep at all, just thinking about becoming full-blown parents the next day and wondering what the baby would be like. Sharlotte and I decided not to ask the doctor what the gender of the baby was during the pregnancy. Therefore, Sharlotte did not know whether the baby was a boy or girl. *I knew, but it was still very exciting to me to keep the secret and share her joy.* We talked and prayed to the Lord and asked Him to deliver us a healthy child. I still remembered my dream and the vision that God showed me in December of 1980. I still had not shared the vision with Sharlotte. I did not feel lead to do so. However, I felt in my spirit that everything was going to be all right. Despite the severe condition of Lupus that Sharlotte endured, and all of the challenges that we had overcome to reach that point in her pregnancy, *the Lord* had delivered us through them all. The news had always seemed to go from bad to worse throughout the final three months of her pregnancy, and there seemed to be no reason for hope from a natural perspective. Nevertheless, *God revealed His faithfulness and power throughout our most challenging moments and we experienced His perfect peace in the midst of our storm!*

Wednesday morning came and the nurses did the final actions to prepare Sharlotte for surgery. We bought a small camera to capture the special moment. We had already decided on a name for the baby, for both genders. If it were a little girl, her name would be *Ebony Nicole Gainous.* If it were a little boy, his name would be *Ramón Christopher Gainous.* When the doctors and surgical team came into the surgery room, the excitement of everything was overwhelming to me. It seemed that everything happened so quickly. Before you knew it, the doctors had delivered the baby and handed her to me! I could not even gather myself to take a picture. Sharlotte had to ask one of the nurses to take some for us! The baby was beautiful! *Ebony Nicole Gainous:*

4 pounds 15-1/2 ounces; 17-1/2 inches long, with a head full of curly black hair! She literally looked like a baby doll! When she was born, she declared her entry into the world with a cry that sounded as if God blessed her with the lungs of a preacher and the voice of a trumpet! *What a glorious sound that was!*

After Ebony was born, they completed the surgical procedure with Sharlotte and moved both of them into the surgical recovery room for a couple of hours before they took them to Sharlotte's room. During that time, I had to complete some hospital paperwork at the nurse's station. While I completed the paperwork, my pastor, Bishop F.D. Lawson, Jr., came into the hospital and met me at the nurse's station. He asked how Sharlotte and the baby were doing and wanted to visit them. L.P. and Arnetta called to inform him that Sharlotte had delivered the baby that morning. I completed the paperwork and led him to the recovery room where Sharlotte and Eb' were. He and I stood at the door of the room and smiled in at them. Sharlotte beamed with pride and joy! She was the mother of a beautiful little girl! Bishop Lawson entered the room, laid his hands upon Sharlotte and the baby and blessed them. His prayer stirred my soul and the Holy Spirit enlightened me of the fact that Bishop Lawson was the older gentleman that I saw in the vision that was in the black suit. My soul rejoiced and I praised the Lord for the fulfillment of His prophecy. Ebony Nicole Gainous was born. The songwriter of *Amazing Grace* eloquently recorded our testimony concerning Sharlotte's pregnancy when he said, *"Through many dangers, toils and snares I have already come; 'Tis grace hath brought me safe thus far, and grace will lead me home."* That is exactly what it was, *God's Amazing Grace! What Joy! What an incredible victory the Good Lord gave to us!* We have kept the whole experience *fresh* in our memories and have shared it as a point of witness and encouragement to the Saints of the Living God throughout my ministry. *Yes, Ebony knows her story! Her life has been a constant witness and confirmation of God's love, power, divine favor and blessings.* She lives in the victory of Jesus Christ, *as a young adult,* and is a strong witness for Him everywhere she goes.

As for that doctor's prediction that Ebony would be mentally retarded, or suffer some sort of serious birth defect, let me share this. Ebony graduated *with honors* from the top-rated public high school in the state of Georgia, *John S. Davidson Fine Arts (Magnet) High School* in Augusta, GA. She is now a *Biology / Pre-Medical* undergraduate student at Howard University in Washington, D.C., pursuing her goal of becoming a Pediatric Physician for the mentally and physically challenged children. *Yes, our life experiences with God, and our wonderful walk with the Lord, have made Sharlotte, Ebony and me CONTENDERS for Jesus Christ!*

My dear friend, if you know that you are a *contestant,* I challenge you to make an eternal decision and commitment to become a *Contender for Jesus Christ!* If you are weak, I encourage you to *get into God's Spiritual Gymnasium, lift those spiritual weights and start executing good spiritual workouts* so that you will become strong in the Lord! Faithfully follow the seven-step spiritual strategy that we outlined in chapter 2. I guarantee it will work for you, and produce the spiritual results that God desires in your life. If you are down, or have been down, because of some personal failure or sin that you have committed in your life, *GET UP and shake yourself right now!* That's right, I am telling you to <u>get over it</u>! *SHAKE IT OFF, PACK IT DOWN, and MOVE ON UP A LITTLE HIGHER!* - Isaiah 55:6-7 says, *"Seek the LORD while He may be found, call upon Him while He is near. Let the wicked forsake his way, and the unrighteous man his thoughts; let him return to the LORD, and He will have mercy on him; and to our God, for He will abundantly pardon." (NKJ) - GET OVER YOUR PAST SINS, GET OVER YOUR PAST FAILURES, and GET ON WITH YOUR LIFE IN THE LORD! GOD has great plans and a bright future for YOU to enjoy! YOU CAN DO IT because "the joy of the Lord is your strength!"* (Ne. 8.10) This is your opportunity to allow the Lord to turn your life around! This is your chance to *rebound* and enjoy a new beginning in the Lord! Jesus will *repair* the broken areas of your life! ***GOD wants to use YOU in His service!***

144

My dear friend, if you are a *Contender for Jesus Christ,* then you are already living a victorious life to the Glory of God! *Bless His Wonderful Name!* However, you cannot be satisfied with your past accomplishments and victories over the devil. You cannot rest on your past laurels because *you have not arrived yet! Heaven is still your ultimate goal!* Subsequently, as long as you are living in this world, there will always be room for you to grow in the Lord's grace and in the knowledge of our Lord and Savior Jesus Christ! *Satan is still your archenemy,* and he is devising a destructive trap that has your name written on it. You must continually *Fight to Win!* Therefore, I challenge you to get stronger and encourage you to *increase your spiritual capacity* by committing yourself to enter a *deeper* relationship with God. Ultimately, your position in the Lord and the service that you render in His name are directly related to your love and passion for Him. The Apostle Paul challenged the saints and faithful brothers in the Colossian church with these words, *"And whatever you do in word or deed, do all in the name of the Lord Jesus, giving thanks to God the Father through Him."* (Col 3:17 NKJ) *DO IT BECAUSE YOU LOVE HIM! Do not compromise your commitment to achieving spiritual excellence in the Lord!*

Today, the Lord is saying YES in your life! *Yes,* you will make it and overcome the devil and sin! *Yes,* you will conquer every obstacle and negative issue that has prevailed in your life to this moment! *Yes,* with God's help, you will overcome every obstacle and negative issue that you will face in the future! *Yes,* you will get beyond the world and its pleasure and live your life to the glory of God! *Yes,* you will increase in the Lord and reach spiritual maturity, by faith! *Yes,* you will fulfill your purpose in the Lord and bless the lives of many! *Yes,* you will surrender the reins of your life to Him and truly allow the Spirit of Jesus Christ to guide and direct you every day! *Yes,* you will remain steadfast in the Lord and *will not compromise* your faith in God! *Yes,* you will *fight and win* to the glory of God! *Yes, YOU WILL ENJOY THE VICTORY because* <u>*YOU ARE A CONTENDER*</u> *AND NOT JUST A CONTESTANT!*